RESILIENCY IN ACTION SERIES

Volume One

But Who's Gonna Wipe Your A**?

An irreverent, honest, and frank look
at midlife and dating after divorce.

ALMA LEIGH

Special dedications and thanks to:

Nick, Avery, Pamela, Alejandra, Candy, Chris, Valerie, Sean, and Aaron as well as all the countless people who have encouraged and supported my endeavors.

Of course, this book would not be possible without the contributions of my clients who willingly volunteered their narratives.

Lastly, a very special dedication to those individuals who came into my life to teach me valuable lessons about integrity, loyalty, honor, honesty, self-love and worthiness. Without you I would not have the depth of empathy and compassion as well as the passionate motivation to put pen to paper. Whether you know it or not, you are the gas to my fire. I appreciate each and every one of you for lessons learned. I have nothing but love for you all!

CONTENTS

INTRODUCTION

Life can be a special kind of hell once we reach middle age. Marriage, divorce, dating, death of our parents and loved ones, adult children, regret, etc.

But Who Is Gonna Wipe Your A** is a frank discussion we all need to have. Many of us go through life living in a bubble of delusion into which we have inadvertently allowed ourselves to fall. That bubble is created from many factors in our lives. Our families, culture, social ties, etc. all have a huge influence in what we do, how we think, feel and act.

There is an incredible amount of pressure that comes from the expectation of how we are to behave. This influence affects the biggest decisions we make in our lives. Midlife tends to be an unintentionally hilarious joke where we have reached a point in critical thinking where we start to really take note of what we've been doing, but more importantly what we need to do next.

So, who's going to wipe your a** at the end of all of this?

When this game ends, who's going to be there for you?

What are you doing right now to subscribe to the investment of these relationships where you will be able to make good sound conscientious decisions to tie up any loose ends?

Are you mentally sound enough to make decisions that are directed towards your long-term wellbeing?

Are you just planning on waiting for the undertaker to decide for you?

Have you given it any thought at all?

Have you, at this point in your life, found that all the romantic relationships you have been involved in are mirror images of one another?

Do you find yourself in superficial connections where you can't even rely upon your romantic partnerships to be a friend?

Do you find yourself fearful of interacting with other people altogether and, as a result, are perpetually on your own?

Do you desire to find companionship, but lack the courage to engage or the know-how to initiate?

My hope is that you read this book and not only figure out what you want to do in the future, but that you enjoy your decisions, particularly if you have been making decisions in the past that were not as well thought out as you would have liked.

I passionately believe that we should enjoy our lives.

Of course, we need to make decisions that are fruitful, productive and provide us with stability and financial resources to have that have an enjoyable outcome. Sometimes those decisions result in us taking a job where we are not necessarily as creative as we would like to be or perhaps we don't receive the level of compensation we feel we are entitled to. We all make tough decisions in life and there's no right or wrong in doing so, as long as it is in alignment with your values.

The question remains, have you taken the time to figure out what your values are? Not the values of your family or your cultural environment, but you as an individual.

What is important to you?

Who are you?

What exactly do you want out of this life and who do you want with you at the end of it?

Who do you trust?

Who are you connected to on the deepest level?

When you get sick, or you are in an accident and are laid up in the hospital, who's going to be there for you?

Hi. My name is Alma Leigh and I'm a licensed clinical social worker. I wrote this book with the intention of affecting people's lives in positive and long-lasting ways. If I have learned anything at all from working with my clients after a divorce or a significant break up, is that no one wants to be alone. Not really. Not long-term.

Most people enjoy solitude after having a tumultuous situation end and that's completely expected and normal. I have had conversations with clients who have expressed a desire to quit dating altogether because, in their mind, they do not see a fruitful outcome no matter which way they look at it.

It is a bit heartbreaking to have a conversation with someone who cannot imagine themselves in a happy and fulfilling connection with another human being. I derive an enormous amount of validation in helping people change their perspective on life and dating. It is a perplexing task, but it's not one that's impossible to achieve.

I, too, am divorced and I am intimately familiar with the trials and tribulations of dating, which is why this subject matter is so close and dear to my heart. I know personally what it is like to get out there again after being in a long term committed connection with another person. I have to say that when you remove yourself from the dating pool for several years and then suddenly you find yourself immersed in unusual and unfamiliar territory, it feels incredibly intimidating. It is not exactly like riding a bike after many years of never riding one, but instead, it's like riding a bike after major hip or leg surgery. Your balance is going to be off if you have not healed.

If you haven't taken the time to heal, you're drastically reducing your chances of engaging in a healthy connection. Hopefully, by reading this book, you will derive some semblance of an idea in which direction you need to take to achieve your own idea of happiness and fulfillment.

Allow me to reiterate, there is no judgement to be had here. In other words, if you have been engaging in fruitless activities involving other human beings, it is important to be aware and mindful of those engagements without the subsequent self-deprecation that comes along with that.

The purpose behind all this work is not to beat yourself up. It is not intended to make you feel bad about yourself. Rather, it is an opportunity to collect evidence of how you are managing your interactions with other people and how those interactions are affecting your life, whether functionally or dysfunctionally.

Look at it this way. If you have a history of cheating in relationships, it is not a benefit to you or anyone else to sabotage future relationships in the same way. It is also not a benefit to blame yourself and label yourself as being a bad person. True, it is injurious behavior to step out of a relationship to which you promised monogamy and fidelity. However, it is critical to isolate the behavior as being an act and not a definition of who you are. This is going to be the first step to healing and change.

A lot of people will engage in hurtful and harmful behaviors to a point where it becomes viewed as a characteristic of that individual's value.

"I'm a cheater."

"I'm a liar."

"I can't be trusted."

"I'm insecure."

"I don't even know what I like in another person."

If a person characterizes themselves in a negative light due to past behaviors, then there is very little motivation to change, particularly if there is a depth of shame associated with these behaviors.

Here is a counter point perspective to that mindset.

It is so simple to characterize the reasons behind the failure of committed relationships as being the fault of the other person. Granted, that is not to discount any failures on the part of previous partners. That is not the purpose of this book. The purpose of this book is to help guide you into your own investigation of your own problematic behaviors. Those behaviors can be outward acts that you engage in with regards to other people or it could be actions that you tolerate.

Some of the stories you will read in this book are difficult. I discuss, in detail, traumatic events that have adversely affected former clients who agreed to share their narrative. I have learned many things in my practice as a psychotherapist. While unfortunate, there is a prevalence of unresolved childhood trauma that adversely affects countless people. Some of the stories in this book will detail these events from the perspective of the client.

Please use discretion in reading these stories, particularly if you have experienced childhood trauma.

Whether or not you have worked on your past trauma, some of the stories in this book can be unsettling. *Please read with caution.*

My hope is that your reason for reading this book is that you have not lost hope. Perhaps you still have hope, but you don't have any real idea of what your future is supposed to look like or even how to manifest change and growth as you move forward in this newly found single existence.

Ultimately, by the time you finish reading this book, I hope that you're able to assess your own habits and your own philosophies in a clear, authentic way without self-deprecation but instead with the ability to articulate where the issue is regarding your personality features that cause you to act, do and say certain things with other people. The long and short of it all is, we do not get into relationships with other people and have those situations dissolve without at least some part being a direct result of our own dysfunctions.

Blame is irrelevant.

At least in regard to how you should move forward in dating. But again, if nothing else, you will enjoy reading the book and it will prompt you to find more avenues to explore in finding out who and what you are at this juncture in your life. I hope you enjoy it and, just remember, it is vital that you simply don't take yourself too seriously. None of us are getting out of here alive.

If you do not bend you'll break.

So be flexible.

Be kind, especially to yourself.

Do the work that you need to do on yourself before presenting into a new connection with someone else.

Enjoy.

CHAPTER ONE

Leaving the past by doing better in the future. The purpose in dating.

This does not have to be heartbreak. This is an adventure.

Perspective is everything.

Let's talk about some uncomfortable truths when it comes to relationships and the expectation of fulfillment from them.

Inherently, we are all alone at any given time.

You have heard it before, but I will say it again. You came into this world alone. You are going to leave this world alone.

Being in a partnership, regardless of how serious it is, will always be a temporary condition.

Most of us have had a handful of relationships. Some of those relationships were positive experiences and, maybe, some of them were traumatic. Some relationships help us grow and some tear us down to our very core. Some relationships affect us so deeply that we feel completely incapable of ever connecting with anyone else. Sometimes, we have so much paralyzing fear that we are unable to even engage in relationships.. Sometimes, we experience a love so deeply that, when it is gone, we simply cannot fathom anyone else taking their place.

Your former partner has likely experienced romantic feelings for other people in the past. Chances are that your past partner will develop an emotional and or romantic connection to a future partner for themselves as well. The sooner you accept this, the sooner your healing can begin. You must understand, it is a normal part of life to have many romantic emotional bonds over our lifespan with many different people. Being married to someone does not negate these emotional bonds for you or your former partner.

You might be wondering what the purpose of this statement is. When someone has a connection to you that is romantic and intimate in nature, it can feel very possessive. Perhaps you feel very possessive of that person. Seeing that person as a human being autonomous of the partnership that you share can be difficult for some people. If it hurts you to consider that your former partner is dating and that is causing you distress, keep in mind that this is a perfect opportunity to figure out what it is about your personality that could adversely affect a future partnership.

For the most part, some jealousy is normal and expected. However, if jealousy has always been a fundamental presence in all your past relationships, then that can be seen as a problematic feature of your own personality. Simply put, being aware of the attractiveness of your partner, or former partner in this case, should initiate some feelings of hesitance or even veiled jealousy, but it should never be a breach or something to create hostility or resentment. That is to say, if your partner or former partner was trustworthy, then they deserve the opportunity to be given that same regard. As we move through these chapters, we will discuss the nuance of trust, both within ourselves and our own behaviors, as well as the expectations from those with whom we connect.

People marry/partner for a variety of reasons. Some of these reasons are logical, fair, and equitable. Some are impulsive and with selfish intention. Some are self-serving and toxic. Some are willfully dedicated and invested. Some are the byproduct of financial necessity. Some are the byproduct of addiction and / or mental health troubles. It is important to understand yourself and what your expectations are in any given dynamic with a partnership. When you understand what your expectations are, then you have the ability to have conversations with a potential partner in the understanding of how you want to potentially move forward in a connection that is mutually beneficial.

The hilarity of it all!

It's kind of funny when you think about it. The idea of wanting to connect and share with someone else and at the end of the day you end up giving more of yourself to that someone. We don't tend to lean into the idea of how much are we willing to sacrifice to be in a partnership. Most of the time, we are considering how that person makes us feel. We want that person to make us feel better about ourselves. We want that person to appreciate our beauty and find us attractive, both intellectually and sexually. We just want to be seen and heard. More often than not, however, we don't tend to think about what our partners needs are before we consider our own. It doesn't mean you're a bad person to feel this way, it just means that you're normal. These considerations are a big purpose in writing this book. It is important to understand the nuances of why we want to be with other people. It is understandable to want other people to have appreciation for us. That is where a lot of betrayal comes into play, if we're honest about it. You must consider the fact that if someone gets into a long-term connection with someone else, and the underpinnings of that connection are tied directly into external validation, then it only makes sense that person would want to reach out to other people as a means to continue that trend. If a person values external validation to the point where they violate the fidelity of their union as a means for that validation, then that is inherently a problem. If this is you, then this is an opportunity for accountable consideration.

Before you can move forward, you must first strip down your last relationship. Think of it as a relationship autopsy. It may get messy, but it is critical to understand what was broken, how it got broken, and how to avoid it breaking down in the future.

Why did you get into a relationship with your former spouse/partner? If you answered because you were in love, I will challenge you to dig deeper. What did being in love look like for you at that time?

You are not a bad person if you admit you wanted financial, physical, emotional, sexual and spiritual safety and security. If you cannot or are unable to admit the real reason you committed to your partner, you won't be able to grow and make better decisions in the future. When we idealize romantic love, we engage in less than forthright behavior. Yes. When we romanticize the idea of being committed we lose sight of pragmatism. We are not able to be as practical and logical as we might if we were to view from an outside perspective. We cannot discern logical, normal, human behavior from intentionally deceitful actions. We start to make everything personal.

What does love look like to you? Better yet, what is your purpose in dating? Why do you want to be with somebody? These can be challenging questions for some people to answer. Not everyone, but most people are uncomfortable admitting their vulnerabilities. When we express a specific desire, it might feel as though other people can see right through us. I do not think anybody wants to be seen as weak. I think it is more difficult for men, culturally speaking, to express a vulnerability regarding the needfulness of companionship or even the desire of intimate love.

We are groomed by culture, by our families, by our friends, and by society, to behave and act in accordance with gender roles. However, it is important to understand ourselves as best as possible before we ever communicate a desire or need to a potential partner. There really should be no shame in doing your relationship forensics and finding out what your personal issues are regarding dating and how you connect intimately with a partner. If you notice a trend and / or your history in dating and relationships having a common theme, well, take a breath, pause briefly and realize that you are the common denominator in that equation.

Again, blame is irrelevant.

Understanding is critical in moving forward. So, I will ask the question again. Think about this before you answer.

What is it that you desire as the outcome of a potential partnership?

The truth is, many people desire partnership, not because they want to be invested or connected to someone else, but it could be a very immature childish need for caregiving. If that is the case for you, then I cannot stress to you how helpful it would be to speak to a mental health provider to better help you navigate the waters of understanding your personality traits. The one thing I am certain of is, you are a normal human being with characteristics that are in alignment with your experiences.

I mean, let's be real. Are you an asshole? Have you been told repeatedly by previous partners that you are selfish or lacking in a particular area? If that is the case, then that's your starting point, my friend. Look at that. Is it true? If it is true, then you have a head start in the game on a direction on what you need to work on. We all have ways that we can improve. We all have ways that we can engage in a committed relationship with someone else that is healthy and reciprocal and provides the partners with the type of support and understanding that would be expected in a productive union.

When you connect with a partner and make a conscientious decision to be in a relationship with that person, there is a certain amount of personal power that you relinquish to that person in good faith and trust that they will not manipulate and use it to their advantage.

Unfortunately, sometimes toxic partners use this position as a measure of control in order to make themselves feel a sense of their own personal empowerment by manipulating yours. Be mindful of this and be careful with who you relinquish your autonomy and power to. This is why when we remove ourselves from toxic situations (all kinds of relationships in fact not just romantic ones), there's a certain feeling of empowerment that comes with that. Sometimes that fulfilled feeling makes us grieve for what we put ourselves through and we have some shame attached to that, even though it is unnecessary. It is important to understand that you just didn't know any better at that time. When you learn you can't continue a relationship with a toxic partner, and you remove yourself from that connection, that feeling of empowerment is something that you should be mindful of. Appreciate the lesson, learn from it, and be mindful of future red flags.

At the end of the day, there is value in understanding who you are. Most of us are so deeply enmeshed in an idea of what we think we are, that it can feel virtually impossible to have an authentic understanding of ourselves on a fundamental level.

The truth is, we are very complex in our own individual ways. We all come from our experiences. Our experiences, both good and bad, provide the template with which our personality develops. We create what we observe whether we do this intentionally or not.

Our behaviors are a direct byproduct of our experiences.

Our sense of self is deeply rooted in how we characterize our worthiness as small children.

These are the threads with which we use to sew together our relationships as adults.

I hope your experience in reading this book provides you with a form of reassurance in understanding that you are not isolated in having feelings of worthlessness, shame, guilt, and insecurity. All human beings deal with these negative aspects at some point. When we are in a loving connected relationship with someone else, these feelings tend to be satiated or eradicated altogether.

Isn't that what we want after all?

CHAPTER TWO

Evolution is a motherfucker.

Evolution makes us do stupid shit to get laid.

Think about it. Looking back in your dating history, what are some things that you might laugh about now but you did as a means to garner the attention of a potential mate? We have gone out on a limb, spent exorbitant amounts of money, made time for people that we should not have made time for, etc. Hindsight is 20/20 indeed! However, it is important to look back on our willfulness and understand why we did what we did. That's how we prevent repeating history. Evolution causes a rush of feel-good hormones when we become sexually aroused. We get high around this person. We get pregnant. Then those hormones stop, and we focus on childcare, building a home and achieving our lifetime goals. While doing the best we can, we achieve this with little to no feedback from the rest of the world. We tend to rely solely on our hormones and our feelings as a means of moving through life. Then we wonder why our relationships don't work.

I can remember being a teenager excited to meet and interact with someone that I chose to focus my romantic attentions. My efforts and energies as a teenager are vastly different than those I possess now in middle age. When I was a young person, I was focused primarily on finding a partner to share my life with that would also be someone who would be a good father and would be able to financially support a growing family. Of course, the trivialization of dating as a teenager was always complicated with superficial desire of attractiveness and physical fitness, and not so much the expectations of intelligence and integrity.

Like many of my peers and clients, I was extremely insecure as a teenager. I was gawky and unusual. I thought that my sense of humor was irreverent and not interesting to my peer group. I was insecure about my facial profile. Often, I would have a self-deprecating internal dialogue reminding myself that I would always be alone because of my unattractive features. Tying this dysfunctional behavior into how I related to potential romantic partners always gives me a sense of malaise or sadness when I think back on those days. I would become irrationally excited when any boy would express an interest in me and, to further complicate the issue, I would immediately dismiss him as a potential partner because, if he held any interest in me, then that meant that something must have been wrong with him! Suffice it to say, I have come along quite a bit since those days. However, when I first got married, I still held onto much of the same mentality. Throughout my marriage and subsequent divorce, I managed to reevaluate those cognitions and see myself as a valuable human being worthy of all the love and life that this universe has to offer. The only real reason I'm sharing this with you is because while yes, I do believe this about myself, I also believe it about you, the reader, as well.

There is absolutely no reason whatsoever why you should go through this life feeling less than or not worthy. If there are things you have done or behaviors you engaged in that are less than savory, then perhaps you need to re-evaluate how you're moving through this life.

Be accountable, change your behavior, dust yourself off and move forward. There is no need to belabor the past to a point where it is suffocating the present and stifling your future. Learn from what you have done in the past, use it for good, and move on in happiness.

Take some time to consider what you think about yourself regarding a relationship. Who are you now? Particularly, who are you now in comparison to who you used to be? You cannot be remotely the same person you were when you first got married or first entered that long term relationship.

Take out a piece of paper or a journal and write down the differences.

Observe them.

Be aware of them.

Be aware of the changes you want to make that you have not achieved. Yes, it is important to understand the type of person you potentially want to connect with. It is equally important to understand the type of person you are as you embark upon this new midlife dating journey. I assume the takeaway from all of this is that you simply do not want to repeat the past. You do not want to move forward in life and wash, rinse, repeat, everything you have done before. Especially if you have not learned any lessons from it. If you have not stopped and taken the time to re-evaluate what has gone on in the past, you are doomed to repeat it. I assume that is not what you want and in fact, you want to succeed in a partnership.

Are there sacrifices you could have made in your past marriage or relationship that you are regretful for not having committed yourself to fully?

Granted, in any relationship dynamic, you always must consider the other person's feelings and how much they're willing to contribute to the rehabilitation of the union. When I ask you to consider any regrets you have, I do not mean for you to engage in some type of re-attack on a previous relationship. The most respectful thing you could do at this point, is to respect your former partner and how they feel and allow things to be as they are. If you have done everything to resurrect and rehabilitate a past relationship, then perhaps it is time to move on and just simply do the forensics in an honest and accountable fashion.

Sit down with your journal.

Write down the things about your past relationship that made you happy in the beginning. What were those things? (Trigger warning: This can be a painful exercise.)

When you sit down and you contemplate how things were in the beginning, it can feel a bit sentimental and can cause the reprisal of painful emotions. Going into this exercise with your journal, it is important to understand that these emotions can happen. Make sure you take some deep breaths and that you understand embarking on this exercise is a logical exploration to simply investigate and nothing more.

What was it about your partner that drew you to them?

Was it purely physical attraction?

Were you enamored by your partner's eyes or their physical shape? It is perfectly OK to admit that your attraction, initially, was physical. It is critical that you understand whether or not your attraction to your partner remained only physical.

What were the features of your partner's personality you found attractive?

What were the red flags you ignored?

How long into the relationship before you had your first fight?

What was it about?

Do you remember why you were angry or why your partner was angry with you?

Walking away from that relationship, do you carry the fixation of blame?

Do you feel like it was your fault the relationship ended?

Do you feel like it was your former partner's fault the relationship ended?

Why do you feel this way? Do not leave it there, though. Keep pressing and keep asking your own questions as a means of unearthing the truth.

When you are honest and authentic with yourself in this exercise, you will reap a bounty of information you can use to grow from in the future. Bear in mind, the way you identify yourself in a relationship, as well as how you value relationships in and of themselves, is a key point of this process.

If you feel a relationship is simply an extension of who you are and a utility to be used as a means of safety and security, then be honest with yourself about that. Chances are, having this knowledge in the future will empower you to be better able to navigate how you move forward in a future partnership. If your potential partner feels that being in a relationship is the most important and vital aspect of their life and you do not share that philosophy, these are critical factors that need to be understood before embarking into a future together. Give yourself the freedom to be honest, both with yourself, as well as with others.

Understand your shortcomings.

Remind yourself that we all have them as a means of relieving yourself of the unnecessary burden of blame and judgement. It is important to know if you were an asshole in a relationship, for sure. But if you do not understand that you are doomed to repeat it. The question is, do you care whether or not you are still an asshole?

A large part of this exploration of who we used to be is critical to understanding the influence of evolution in that process. You are not the same person you were when you first got into that relationship, as I have said before. Your motivations now are likely to be vastly different than they were when you were a teenager. Your efforts in dating were highly influenced by the flux of testosterone and / or estrogen.

Young people seek partners to procreate with at a basic level. Of course, being a horny teenager, many of us were not trying to get someone pregnant or get pregnant. However, the desire for having sex with someone is inherently a fundamental component of reproduction. Those hormones are what causes us to have those sexual desires and thus, engaging in sexual behaviors. Evolution has enslaved the human brain with feel good hormones that, for some, can only be accessed through sexual excitement. Finding a partner that excites us sexually can cause us to engage in a myriad of responses and actions that we might not necessarily engage upon without the activation of those synapses. More than likely, now that you are middle aged and you've already experienced marriage and / or long-term commitment, your mindset is most likely very different than it was 20-something years ago.

However, with the increasing evolution of scientific break-throughs regarding reproduction, people are growing more comfortable waiting until later in life to start their families. With that said, only you can decide what your motivations are in dating at this point in your life. I realized authoring this book that my narrative is not necessarily the narrative of my contemporaries. I have already had the children I am going to have in this life and I am quite comfortable in moving forward, looking for companionship that makes me feel safe in a variety of ways, without the expectation or desire of starting a family.

Figure out who you were back then. Identify and chronicle what you wanted at that point in your life. Now ask your present self the same questions and compare how much you have changed. Isolate the reasons for those changes. Consider and meditate upon all this newfound information as a means of laying the groundwork for the foundation of a healthy and prosperous future in a partnership that is both gratifying and rewarding.

True, as human beings there are aspects of the human experience that are quite common and make us all remarkably similar. However, as individuals go, we have all had different experiences and we have different goals. It is vital to understand what your intentions are moving forward. Not everyone wants the same thing, particularly when it is regarding the outcome of any relationship.

What are your interests? What are your dealbreakers? What is it about you that you would not want to see as a personality feature in a potential partner? What do you already know about yourself that you want to grow from or change?

Midlife dating after divorce or breakup is a complete juxtaposition to dating before marriage or long-term commitment in your teens and early 20s, no doubt. We all grow. Some of us evolve at a much faster rate than others, but I believe it is a safe assessment to say that a person in their late 40s and early 50s is vastly different than the person they were in their 20s, or at least I would hope they are!

The priorities you faced as a 20-something looking for a lifetime partner are likely very different now in mid-life. Motivations, hopes, dreams and aspirations evolve over time, particularly if goals have already been achieved. While being midlife has the added benefit of life wisdom, you must also accept that the additional years bring with it the chaos of a life fully lived. Trauma, loss, and pre-existing mental health conditions tend to be fairly normal for midlife divorced people. If you have survived this far, it's likely because you have experienced adversity. Being mindful of the fact that experiencing adversity and accepting it as part of life as opposed to something to be avoided, will alleviate any expectations of a perceived perfect person. Instead, having this understanding will provide you with the ability to focus more on the connection itself, as opposed to the people within that connection. Whether or not you are compatible with someone has little to do with how old they are, but more to the point of how resilient they have been through the adversity that they have undoubtedly faced.

Not only are we evolutionary creatures as human beings, but we also must take into account the evolution that we encounter as individuals throughout our lives. We must understand that change is a factor and is a normal component of the human experience. I would even go one step further to assert that this evolution of the individual is a key point in the breakdown of marriages, fundamentally.

People change.

People grow.

Sometimes that growth causes a disconnect in relationships, resulting in a breakup. If we are capable of understanding that growth and change is expected over time, then we tend to have the ability to be more accepting of those changes as opposed to defending against them. This creates resiliency in any partnership.

Sometimes ending a romantic partnership is unavoidable due to personal growth and change.

After all, isn't it possible to break up with a romantic partner but maintain a friendship and mutual respect? If that is the end result, is it a breakup after all?

Is it more of a transition of a friendship? My interpretation of a breakup is a complete and total dissolution with no contact afterwards. If two people come together in a romantic partnership and create a commitment together which ultimately falls apart for whatever reason and those two people are capable of maintaining a mutually respectful friendship, then I don't see that as a breakup at all, but a transition. This transition opens up opportunities for the individuals in that relationship to seek romantic connections elsewhere. It's all about perspective.

The all-or-nothing mentality of relationships can be over-whelming. When you think back on the breakdown of your past relationships, and you remember the sadness that you feel in the disconnect, perhaps this is an opportunity to reframe that somewhat.

It is the normal evolution in relationships.

We all evolve and grow and, as a result, our needs and desires change.

Once we realize we have outgrown a particular relationship in its original inception, then we can attempt to at least assert the introduction of a new definition of what that relation-ship is. All of this to say is, it is only possible when respect and trust are intact. That is why accountability is key in the dissolution of any relationship. I cannot imagine dissolving a partnership with someone without at least attempting to maintain respectful civility. It is not always possible, but it's always worth trying.

CHAPTER THREE

Understanding the serial dater: Lamar's story

There are endless reasons why someone would perpetually seek out brand new and exciting partnerships with unknown individuals. There is a sense of safety connecting with someone whom you do not share a committed relationship. The normal mundane tasks and responsibilities of everyday life are not a key factor in the initial excitement of meeting someone new. The allure and fantasy of an initial engagement with someone can often feel like a drug with a similar effect on the brain. The addictive nature of these engagements can often inhibit someone from engaging in longer term connections. The lack of depth and superficial nature of these short-lived rendezvous is replaced with a fantasy of an exciting, often overtly sexual, albeit short-term engagement.

For the midlife, divorced dater, this can become a problem. Similar to a drug addiction, changing up a particular habit cultivated from a need to derive excitement can be virtually impossible. More often than not, the serial dater does not want to stop dating new and exciting people.

I have never interviewed a divorced person in midlife who did not express some experience of a deeply painful heart-break. Using this logic, I would surmise that serial dating is a trauma response to heartbreak. Additionally, the heartbreak is not always a romantic one. Many people after divorce and breakup, and after some significant therapy work, are able to identify the root wound they experienced.

Parental abandonment is a prevalent wound that many people exhibit when engaging in therapeutic process. For the average person, it does not make a whole lot of sense to connect the fact that a child who has experienced parental abandonment would exhibit the features of fear of commit-ment later on in life. Most people don't understand how parental abandonment can influence future romantic partnerships. However, it is a key factor in many folks who demonstrate insecurities regarding the connections they attempt to create in their adult life. Think about it. It makes a lot of sense to consider that a child who experiences the abandonment of a parent or caregiver will ultimately develop a personality trait that is fearful of experiencing that level of pain again. Anytime there is an emotional attachment to any other person, romantic or otherwise, creates a vulnerability for that pain to emerge. Therefore, the adult child who experienced a significant abandonment wound would naturally want to seek out superficial relationships where there is no expectation of an emotional investment long term.

Theoretically, this eliminates the potential for any abandonment when there is no emotional attachment to begin with.

Aside from the avoidance of triggering an old attachment / abandonment wound is the allure of the chase. It is exciting to feel that initial attraction to someone. For some, having lived half of their life in a state of survival when it comes to the emotional attachment to other people, the initial gratification of engaging a stranger in a proposition for immediate comfort and connection can be just as unavoidable as the drug addict is unable to turn down using their drug of choice.

Understanding is half the battle. Here is an analogy to better illustrate these behaviors.

Have you ever been driving down the road and up ahead you see the bright lights of emergency services vehicles? As you are getting closer you cannot help but pay attention to what's going on the side of the road. You see the flashing lights and your curiosity grows as you drive closer. The concept of "rubbernecking" comes from the turning of the head and paying attention to something that's going on in the peripheral as opposed to paying attention to the direction that you're heading in. We see the lights. They are bright and flashing. How can we ignore that? This metaphor serves two purposes. The first is the mentality of the serial dater. That person who cannot seem to commit to one individual because they're consistently distracted by everything else going on around them. Midlife serial daters can be particularly toxic. There can be the added mentality of "fear of missing out". Driving past such a spectacular sight such as a vehicle accident with all the lights flashing, can be a daunting task for somebody who struggles with the ability to focus and / or commit. That neck turns into rubber and flashing lights and sirens are a call to any person who is fearful of not knowing what is happening over there. Midlife serial daters are very much like this. They have, by default, ingrained upon themselves a mentality based upon the perceived isolation and dullness of their past committed relationship or relationships. Serial daters are not necessarily bad people, nor are they people that should be avoided in dating. What is critical is to understand who and what you are dealing with when you meet a serial dater. Understanding your own personal boundaries when it comes to the interaction with people in general is critical and key if you are dating. Ask questions. Ask them what they are looking for and hold space for your own interpretation of what they are saying to you because often, with the serial dater, they will simply project what it is they think you want to hear as a means of attaining their own goal, which normally results in sex. There is no judgment in having sex with someone, particularly if it's a casual arrangement that has been discussed and communicated fully. The damage comes from the expectation of a long-term emotional connection when there is no intention on the part of the serial dater.

If you understand that effectively, then metaphorically, you are that fire engine with its lights flashing. Because of your presentation, you give off a surface level attraction to the serial dater.

It is nice to be desired, isn't it? It's nice to know that, regardless of whether or not someone wants to have a long-term relationship with you, at least they do find you physically attractive which, for the most part, in midlife that in and of itself can be hugely rewarding. In midlife we have had children, we've suffered the slings and arrows of time, weight gain, and weight loss. Our bodies have aged. We are not the young, vibrant, youthful and fit beings we once were many years ago.

Perhaps you are the serial dater.

Maybe you feel like something's wrong with you? Maybe from a cultural perspective, you feel like you need to be more focused on finding a partnership, which is what the title of this book implies.

Being a person in the dating game who is easily distracted from one person to the next, while in the moment, can be mutually gratifying. The experience of dating and / or having casual sex with numerous partners can simply be just an evolution of ensuring you have sown your oats properly after leaving a long-term committed relationship, before entering into a new partnership. You, your potential partner

,or perhaps, the both of you feel the need to evolve sexually by having several sexual partners. If you are, in fact, dating a serial dater, what is your desired outcome? Are you being rational and reasonable in your expectations?

Are you setting yourself up for heartbreak because you have this expectation that they will see you as the one person with whom they choose to commit?

Are you the serial dater and do you feel regret or shame in your behaviors?

Do you have several casual sexual partners and not feel any emotional connection at all?

It is all about understanding what you're doing and why you're doing it.

Blame is irrelevant.

You may just be merely scratching an itch at this point in the game. If you are informing your potential sexual partners of your intentions and you are subscribing to a healthy mindset regarding emotional, as well as sexual and physical health, then you shouldn't worry about anything other than whether or not your actions have merit.

At the end of the day, what is your goal with regard to all of these encounters?

What benefit do they bring to your life?

Are you merely avoiding the fear that you experience in being vulnerable with a potential partner?

Are you dating a serial dater with the expectation that you're going to win his or her affection long term?

The end game in all of this is to be accountable for your own behavior and what you bring to the table in these engagements, as well as being rational about why you're engaging in it to begin with.

Are you kicking rocks, wasting time and avoiding dating for partnership?

Do you even believe that there is a potential person out there for you that you can connect to emotionally, intellectually and sexually?

Are you content looking off in the periphery and allowing yourself to be distracted by those flashing lights?

What is the end goal?

Lamar has been married to Yin for 25 years. They met in college at a fraternity house party. Lamar remembered seeing Yin standing in the corner next to her friends quietly sipping out of a cup of stale house beer.

"She was the most exquisite and exotic looking creature I had seen in quite a long time. She had this beautiful jet-black hair with eyes to match. She didn't look like any of her sorority sisters and yet she seemed to be blithely unaware of her beauty. She wasn't at the party trying to get the attention of all the other guys either. She was just there because her sorority sisters encouraged her to put her books down and to come and hang out with the rest of the girls. She was a virgin. I took her virginity that night. She was very sweet about it, but I could tell that she was also very uncomfortable the next day. I took her out to coffee and that was when we started dating seriously. She never questioned anything. She was always available. She never played games with me. I was never worried that she was going to cheat on me. I was always screwing other girls. The whole time we dated, I was still out running around on Yin."

"Did you ever feel bad about cheating on your wife?"

"Well, she wasn't my wife back then. This was when we were dating."

I looked at Lamar and cocked my head to the side "Did you ever feel bad about cheating on your wife?" I inquired a second time.

Lamar shifted uncomfortably in his chair and stiffened his jaw while looking at me. "I know what I did. I know it was dirty. If you're trying to make a point, then you've made it. I already feel bad enough, as it is."

"I'm not trying to make you feel anything, Lamar. I am just asking you the question. At any point in time, when you were cheating on your wife or then-girlfriend, did it ever occur to you to have any kind of guilt or shame or regret about cheating on her?"

Lamar huffed and squirmed a bit in his chair. He looked around the room seemingly for answers. "I probably should have. But no. I didn't. I didn't care. I think part of me felt like she didn't care either because she never asked me about it. She never got jealous. She never asked where I was. I think she knew but she just never said anything. So, I just kept doing it."

"What are you feeling right now, having this conversation with me, Lamar? I'm not trying to make you feel bad, but the purpose of this therapy is for you to really understand yourself and your motivations as a means to heal and grow and move forward."

"I guess I feel a little bit attacked by you. I think if you were in my head, you would know that I am my own worst critic. I mean, I am like really awful to myself. If I am being completely honest, I know that I never deserved to be with Yin to begin with. She should have married someone else. She should never have married somebody like me. I was not a good boyfriend and I was not a good fiancé and I damn sure was not a good husband. I make good money. I pay all the bills. She never really had to work and so she never really learned how to work and take care of herself. Now I get to pay the price for everything that I have done. She threw her life away to be with me and I just took it. I just took her love.

I took everything for granted. She is agreeing to this divorce because I'm asking for it. She never argues anything. She just lets me have my way. I told her that I cheated on her because she would not have sex with me. The truth is she would have never been able to satisfy my appetite. I cheated on her because I did not want her. I wanted something else. I was always wanting something else or someone else. She did not want to have sex with me because she was disgusted with me because she knew I was cheating on her. Now I am the one leaving. Now I am the one abandoning her. I know it is hurting her, but she won't tell me because she doesn't want to hurt me. She has always put my feelings ahead of her own. I don't know what to do now, because I feel so horrible and worthless that I can't even look at myself in the mirror. That's how I'm feeling right now. That's how I feel all the time. I don't think that you should try to make me feel any different because I deserve to feel this way. I deserve this special brand of hell. My kids hate me too and I deserve that too."

"So why don't you stay and try and work it out?"

`"Part of me feels like I owe it to her to let her go. The selfish part of me wants to just be free and fuck as many women as I possibly can, because that's the only thing that really makes me feel anything close to being alive. When I'm around some-one I don't know, and they don't see the real me, I feel, for just a brief moment, that I'm normal and OK. But they always find out who I am, Alma. They always figure out that I'm not going to stick around as soon as they know who they're dealing with. Then I get back on the dating apps and I find somebody else. Financially speaking, I will always take care of Yin and she knows that. I wish that she would be able to support herself, but I know the reason I wish that is so I wouldn't feel so bad about pulling her away from her friends in college and taking her out of school and getting her preg-nant for five years of her life. She never finished college. I did. I got my degree. I went back and got my MBA. She made it three years in undergrad and dropped out when we got married. So, now she cleans houses just like her mother did. Her parents came to America hoping for a better life for her and this is what she gets. A cheating asshole of a husband."

"You know, if I were crazy, Lamar, I would say that you almost sound like you're feeling a little bit sorry for your-self. Why is that? Keep in mind I'm not judging you I'm just asking a question."

"I don't know. Maybe because I am just a piece of shit. Maybe because I cannot control my impulses and I end up hurting every person that I interact with. I know that I never deserved a woman like Yin to begin with. I know that there is something wrong with me, but I do not know how to fix it. I do not even know if it can be fixed. I don't know if I deserve to be fixed."

"Have you ever taken the time to journal and sit down and just write out what you would like your life to look like ideally? Do you think that is something you could try to do?"

"I think it's a little bit late for that, don't you?"

"Not necessarily Lamar. Whether or not your marriage, at this point, is salvageable is irrelevant to the question. Regardless of what happens in your relationship with Yin, you still need to figure out why you are behaving this way."

"Ideally? Ideally, I wouldn't be so fucking scared all the time. Ideally I wouldn't feel so fucking worthless. Ideally, I would have a friend group that I could connect with and feel commonalities with and not feel like the outcast all the time. I feel like I have to be the comedian in the group so I can fit in. I have never felt like I fit in with anyone. I have always been an anomaly in any setting. I have never felt like just by being me, that I was worth enough. I became extremely competitive as a means to justify my existence in school and in life, in general. Yet this fear is always with me. It is like a yoke around my neck. On one hand, I am responsible for everyone around me and, on the other hand, I feel like I am a complete and total joke of a man. I feel like people see through me. When they see through me, I am done with them. I cannot handle it. That is why me and Yin have lasted for so long. She's never questioned me. She's never made me feel like I've hurt her, even though I know I have. She's always just let me do everything I wanted to do and even that wasn't enough! Hell, I have resented her for years for not standing up to me! Part of me wanted her to fight with me so that maybe fighting with her would help me change how I was treating her. But I know it's not her fault. I've always just kind of treated people like shit because I've always felt like shit. I've always used people because I felt like that was the only way I was ever going to get any kind of connection with anyone else, because I wasn't worth anything else. I'm a piece of shit, so why not act like one?"

"Lamar, do you want to change your behavior? It is a fair question. Step outside of your cognitions of yourself. Set aside the belief that you think you are a worthless piece of shit for just a moment. I want you to consider whether or not you want to change."

"Whoa, Alma that's a hard one. It is hard to set aside that belief. I guess so. I mean who does not want to do better? Who doesn't want to become an ideal version of himself? Yes, I do want to change. But wanting to change and believing that it's possible are two different things. You should know that."

"Well, I do believe that it's two different things. However, you must understand that I don't see you the way you see yourself. Your cognitions are vastly different than my observations of you. I do not have any type of agenda or emotional attachment to creating a narrative that is inaccurate as far as how I see you. Granted, I can sit here and tell you what I think about you, but because of your cognition of self, you're not likely to believe me. The fact is, you must do the work yourself if you are going to change your behavior. I can provide you with the skills and the tools to engage in this introspection of self. That is the basis of cognitive behavioral therapy. You must be aware of what your cognitions are to address them and then, ultimately, to affect positive change."

"So, do you think with this kind of therapy that I can become a perfect husband, fix my marriage, and make everybody happy all the time and feel good about myself? Is that it?"

"No, but ultimately reframing your cognitions into a healthier and more rational perspective will provide you with the understanding of why you engaged in dysfunctional behaviors in the past and then you will be better able to combat those issues in a healthier way in the future. The outcome of that is up to you. Whether there is any opportunity for reestablishing this connection with your wife is irrelevant to whether or not you need to make these efforts. You must take care of yourself simply because that's what you need to do. You never want to engage in a therapy setting or a period of growth or change with the expectation of a particular outcome, specifically when your efforts are targeted to changing the nature of a relationship. If you are willing and able to make changes without an attachment to an outcome, then ultimately the positive effect of your changes will create positive outcomes, regardless of what they may be. In other words, you can't focus on whether or not this is going to save your marriage. You just have to focus on it because you deserve to understand who and what you are and why you think and feel in such negative terms. You must understand why your belief about yourself causes you to behave in such dysfunctional and harmful ways. You also must do all of this without beating yourself down in self-deprecating ways. One of the hardest things my clients have to do in this process is to accept themselves at face value without affixing a value toward themselves with regard to their behavior. True, you have been acting in shitty ways. A lot of what you're telling me is really awful, deplorable behavior. What I am saying to you is that your deplorable actions are just that. They are actions. You are not a deplorable person unless you choose to continue engaging in deplorable behaviors. You have a choice, Lamar. I just don't know if you realize that just yet. That's why you need to start the journaling. I cannot sit here and journal for you. You must come to terms with what your truth is."

"I want to change. Sitting here in your office, I feel inspired to be a better man. But I know as soon as I leave your office today and I go out to my car and I see some hot woman getting into her vehicle, I'm going to start fantasizing and challenging myself as to whether or not I can get her number and then, after that, I'm going to challenge myself to see if I can get her to go out to lunch with me and then, after that, I'm going to see how long it's going to take me to get her to sleep with me. What about that? That feels really good to me. Knowing that I can talk to a woman and get her to have sex with me within one or two dates is an incredible ego boost. I love it. I love that kind of attention. You are telling me that I have to give that up in order to become a better man? I don't know if I can do that. It feels too good to have that kind of validation. It almost makes it worth being such a piece of shit. That's why I do it."

"Why do you think it feels good, Lamar?"

Lamar busted out laughing. "You're joking right? "

"No." I responded flatly. " It's a serious question."

"It feels good because it just fucking does! I mean for me; I didn't talk to girls when I was in school. I was fucking terrified. I was always scared. Hell, I'm still scared! It's the only way I can get outside of that fear is to challenge myself to do something that will help me to not feel so afraid, if only for just a short amount of time. Man, they love me too! I know it is wrong. I say things to get them to sleep with me. I tell them that I have love for them. I tell them that I can see me being their husband. That is why I'm a piece of shit, because I say shitty things that I don't mean. Then I sleep with them, then

I stop talking to them, then they go crazy, and then I tell them the reason I don't talk to them is because they're crazy and I just try to get rid of them. When I say it out loud, it sounds a lot worse than it really is."

"I don't know, Lamar. It sounds pretty horrendous, what you're doing. I also think you know it and I think that each and every time you do this to people, it makes you feel worse and worse about yourself. I think that while you do derive an immediate sense of gratification and validation in having sex with these women, I think on the other end of it you realize what you've done and how you have to sort of massage these connections so that you don't feel so bad when you finally do disconnect from them. I do not think you really know what it feels like to just be OK and not need that constant validation. That is the nature of this work. That is where you are going to get a benefit. If you can figure out that you are worthy and that you are a special kind person with a huge creative ability and see yourself the way other people see you, you won't need that immediate sense of validation and gratification. It will not have the same pull if you can manage to see yourself the way other people see you."

"And how is that, Alma, because I have no idea what other people see. I think I'm a good-looking man. I've been told that time and time again. I've taken some photographs and I've done some modeling. I'm pretty confident in my appearance. But aside from everything else, I don't think I have a whole hell of a lot to offer besides a lot of pain to whomever comes into my world."

"Well, I see a very scared individual. I see somebody who feels lost. I also see someone who feels compelled to withhold and repress his own pain because of the roles he is in as a husband, father and professional. I do not feel like you can talk to anybody. I do not think you're even that comfortable talking with me. I just understand how experiences in childhood affect the development of our personality and our mannerisms and how we engage other people. Who hurt you? Because I don't think that you would be acting this way and treating other people this way if you didn't have a wound that you were trying to fix or heal in some dysfunctional fashion. Think back on it. Dig deep. If you had to answer in a knee jerk response, who hurt you? Who gave you your wound? That's what you're going to have to journal. That is what you're going to have to face. The fear that you feel now, as a man, is a direct response to your avoidance of that very question. When you face that and you acknowledge it, you will see that it will be the foundation to your healing journey. You cannot heal if you do not acknowledge what broke you. So, what was it, Lamar? What happened to you?"

"I can't say anything bad about my dad. He has been dead for a long time. He taught me a lot. He spent a lot of time with me. I would not have a lot of the skills I have if it weren't for him."

Lamar looked at the floor and began to weep.

"I never felt like I was good enough in his eyes. He loved me one minute and the next minute, he hated me."

Lamar looked up at me with red eyes. "All I ever wanted was his approval. All I ever wanted was to feel loved by him. Sometimes he would spend time with me and it was wonderful. I paid close attention to everything he ever showed me. I only wanted to make him proud of me. Most of the time, I felt like I was in the way. Especially when he would have friends over. He never wanted me around. I was just this dumb little kid who got under his feet. I never felt like I was enough in the eyes of my father."

"You do realize this is the beginning of your journaling journey right? You know that this is what you need to address as you are moving forward in your healing?"

Lamar nodded his head in agreement.

Over the next 18 months Lamar experienced a tremendous amount of emotional growth. His divorce was completed with Yin, but they remained friendly. When he was ready, Lamar sat down with his wife and confessed to her all his infidelities. Per her usual performance, Yin expressed compassion and understanding. She expressed forgiveness and thanked him for his honesty but did not express any outward concern or conflict or even an expression of her own injury because of his behaviors. Lamar accepted this at face value and did not question or expect any other reward.

At the end of 18 months, Lamar and I terminated our therapeutic relationship. He was leaving his job and was planning to travel alone. He had also ended a relationship with a woman that he had been casually seeing for four years. He apologized to her, but then stated that he needed to date himself for a while.

"I've got some travel plans coming up and I'm excited about that. This is the first time that I've ever gone on a trip by myself without the intention of getting laid. I want to do some backpacking and I want to do some rock climbing. I just need to be alone for a while. I need to get to know myself. It'll be good."

Lamar took some time to travel and to write. He checks in routinely with me, although we never reconnected in a client therapy relationship. He remains single and abstinent. He states that sex is no longer a priority but being mindful of his impact on the emotional well-being of those around him is.

The truth of the matter is, in all of this you, and you alone, hold the power in how you move through your life in all of your relationships.

Those bright flashing lights make those hormones go off in your brain but, beyond that, do you still keep moving forward until you see the next collection of flashing lights?

Will you continue driving?

Do you know where you are driving?

Leaving a long-term relationship or marriage means a lot of different things for a lot of different people. More often than not, the marriage or relationship that failed, did so for many different reasons. However, the feeling of entrapment or imprisonment is often a predominant factor. Feeling withheld and unable to live your life on your terms because of a promise made years ago can be suffocating. Just like with any trauma, the post effects of that experience are hugely involved in the actions that take place in the now. The serial dater, who left a long-term relationship or marriage, quite possibly fears ever returning to that type of a commitment at any point in time, ever. So as a means to have needs met for connection, albeit superficial in its sexual nature, the serial dater will do what they have to do in order to achieve their needs in the moment.

Perhaps it's the actualization of a fantasy that played in the serial dater's mind when they were married.

"If I wasn't in this situation right now, I would be sleeping with all kinds of men / women."

Many midlife separated or divorced, serial daters see themselves as actualizing a fantasy. Perhaps they got married at a young age and they weren't able to do the things that they desired or perhaps they had too much fear or insecurity to date more before they chose to get married or commit to a long-term relationship. There are endless reasons for people to want to date casually.

Are you a serial dater?

If so, why? More to the point, if you are a serial dater and you are reading this book are you seeking answers on how to evolve out of this behavior? It must be a daunting fear to challenge one's own thinking about dating, regarding long term commitment, especially when your past experiences with long term commitment have not been positive. It is hard to hold hope for the future when you look in the past and see regret and failure. May I suggest that this book is a tool to help you evolve and explore your mentality and your cognitions about your past relationship or relationships? Just because you've experienced turmoil in the past, is not a guarantee that turmoil awaits you in the future.

Just like driving down that road and seeing the flashing lights on the side of the road that draw your attention, you can also realize that you are on a path by staring at the flashing lights as a distraction and nothing more.

You can observe the elation of what the flashing lights do to your brain without engaging upon the involvement of pulling your car over and getting out and staring at the lights and connecting with the lights and wasting your time on your journey with something that is only temporary in its reward. You can choose to remind yourself that the reason you are driving to begin with is because you do have a destination. As you move forward on your journey, you realize the direction that you're going in now is vastly different than the one you embarked upon several years ago that led you into that unfulfilling relationship.

It is OK to feel fear.

It is OK to be vulnerable.

It's OK to feel the shame of feeling like you failed.

When you understand you have the ability to allow yourself to feel, you will be far less likely to be distracted by the peripheral events that are simply not part of your goal. The question remains.

Are you driving so that you can find all of these different flashing lights or are you driving because you desire to be somewhere that you've never been?

CHAPTER FOUR

Why do we keep screwing up?

But seriously. What exactly are you doing as you move through this life in your attempts to find suitable companionship? The things I have observed, not only in my own experiences, but looking around and seeing broken homes by the thousands, has me completely baffled as to why we have not only failed in relationships, but we failed ourselves. These relationships bring children into the world and in their faltering create discontent, trauma, abandonment, and a variety of other lingering mental health conditions that can last throughout a lifetime.

Through that observation, I've concluded that perhaps, if we as individuals took time to consider what exactly it is we are longing for in our attempts to find companionship, then perhaps on the other end after finding companionship, we may have better success in maintaining those healthy relationships or at least in building something worthwhile and long lasting.

Not all relationships end in disaster. Some wind down overtime and come to an amenable conclusion. Some end after many years together with the finality of exhaustion and not having any more lingering fight left in them. One thing that we must consider, if we are going to actualize as individuals, existing as autonomous people within the constraints of a committed and healthy union with someone else, is this point alone.

Every relationship ends.

However, the consideration that it takes in order to ensure a relationship is fruitful and honest and provides support, love, compassion, and consideration that we all generally want, is a goal. However, it is a goal I don't think many of us seriously, or consciously, consider. Or we do take it seriously and, as a result, we find these considerations incredibly fearful and we find a huge chasm of self-doubt and low self-worth to the point we wonder if we are lovable by someone else at all.

So, the real question here, is why do relationships end?

Well, the first answer to that is death of one of the partners. The next answer is divorce. For the most part though, the majority of marriages end over some kind of battle with regards to sex and / or money, or a combination of both. Whether it's one or both of the partners engaging in extra-marital affairs or perhaps mismanaging money or perhaps not earning enough money. Criminal behavior, child abuse and domestic violence are all factors that can also play into the dissolution of these unions.

Let us dig a little deeper.

If someone engages in abuse, whether that is emotional, physical or both, is it the result of a lack of investigation or due diligence on the part of the other partner?

Did the partner know, that entering into this relationship with this person, these behaviors existed and perhaps they turned a blind eye?

Maybe they thought that once they became married, the negative behaviors would end or lessen.

Or perhaps they had no idea and they married someone they really did not know. Often, people who engage in manipulative tactics, do so from a place of very careful consideration as a means to ensure their needs are always met by their partner. Unfortunately, this kind of manipulation normally manifests in a fashion that does not allow room for authenticity. Lies, deceit, and betrayal often follow and once the partner has had enough and leaves, then the relationship ends.

What causes these kinds of behaviors? Do people grow up in abusive homes or neglectful environments and become awful, terrible, excuses of human beings and try to cover who they are until they are able to secure a partner they can manipulate and take advantage of?

Many times, small children who have had to exist in adverse conditions, adapt to their environment by becoming equally manipulative and, as a result, they grow into adults who do not have the ability to navigate their environment under authentic conditions and behaviors.

Truth is, some people do not have the capacity for authenticity and honesty simply because they've been conditioned to do exactly the opposite.

How do these people end up in relationships?

How do these people continually move through life utilizing tactics that are obviously not working long term?

They find themselves entering into another relationship and yet another relationship, until finally they're in their midlife, alone and terrified for what the future may hold.

CHAPTER FIVE

Taking time to heal: Rob's story

How long has it been? How long should you wait to date after a significant break up? Just like with many other situations in life, there is no specific timeline that anyone person should adhere to when it comes to moving forward in life. However, most of us probably would not consider signing up for a marathon immediately after getting over food poisoning.

Rationally, we all know that it takes time for our body to bounce back from a significant illness. For some strange reason, whether it be cultural, societal, or just a generalized sense of expectation, we don't give the same grace toward our emotional health as we do our physical condition.

Our psychological needs mirror our physical needs in many ways. However, for some reason, culture dictates that it is only acceptable to recuperate after physical illness. Perhaps, it is the ability to visually observe an injury. We cannot see emotional illness. We cannot see someone's mental instability. We cannot see the grief, depression and / or anxiety that resides in the hearts, minds, and spirits of those around us.

We tend to invalidate what we cannot observe.

That, of course, culminates in the collective mentality that emotional illness and injury must be something to be hidden and / or addressed on your own time, without any perceivable display of a problem to others around you. Of course, I share this with you as a point of validation in that you must heal. Experiencing a breakup, regardless of your level of emotional investment within that dynamic or for your previous partner, is a personal evolution. Everyone's experience in breakups is different.

However, one factor remains the same and that is you are now affected by that breakup. The amount of time you need to recover is dependent upon the level of injury you sustained from the relationship, as well as the separation. The question now is to determine whether or not your desire to date is based upon your need for healthy connection or are you looking for some type of emotional prop to help you move out of your emotional illness and / or injury. Think of it like this. If you have not healed from the insults and injuries of your past relationships, then you are going to look for ways to provide some type of comfort for the pain that still exists. Think of it as a broken leg. If you break your leg and you don't go to the doctor and you simply stay at home and wrap it up yourself, you might possibly get lucky and manage to heal on your own without any type of medical intervention, but for the most part, I think we can all agree that a broken leg needs some type of intervention in order to properly heal for your long term health, wellness, flexibility, and mobility.

So, for instance, you could consider medical intervention, such as x-rays and a cast on your leg, equivalent to taking the time you need after a breakup to heal, as well as talking to a therapist about your experience in that relationship, and how the breakup affected you.

Dating immediately after a significant breakup is much like climbing onto the back of someone else and expecting them to carry you around. I mean, sure, you could meet someone who would be more than happy to pick you up and put you on their back. It happens all the time in codependent relationships. However, you lose your autonomy by climbing on to the back of someone else and do not possess the ability to stand on your own. Additionally, investing your time in a codependent relationship will only further the time needed to heal properly.

How long has it been since your breakup?

Are you mourning the loss of this relationship?

Breakups are incredibly painful, in a big part, due to the confusion that it brings. Much of the hardship can be attributed to the conflict between your logical assessment of the situation versus your emotional experience. Emotionally, you may be sitting with the feelings that you miss this relationship and this person terribly. However, logically, you know that this person is not good for you. You can love someone and miss them and, at the same time, know that being with them is not right for your health and wellness long term. That is why taking time for yourself is so critical at this point. It is incredibly important to be able to honor and grieve your feelings. If you jump out of one relationship and immediately start dating other people, you will be happy in the moment, for sure. There is a lot of really interesting and intriguing people out there in the world. Connecting with someone, even short term, can make you feel some relief of that pain. Bear in mind, connecting to someone else before you have fully healed and release the connection from your previous relationship, is akin to addictive behavior. You are simply using an immediate connection with someone else as a method of temporarily stopping the painful feelings that you need to be processed.

Perhaps this isn't the first time you've been down this road. More often than not, middle-aged folks have been in more than one committed relationship over a long period of time. Keeping this in mind only further magnifies the need for some self-imposed solitude, as well as consulting with a professional mental health counselor.

After all, it can be a hard pill to swallow realizing you are the common denominator. It can be incredibly shameful and triggering to confront your own demons about how you move through relationships. However, I would like for you to take a moment to consider a few things. A big part of the shame response when we feel like it is us:

Maybe I am the problem.

Maybe I am the reason that my relationships don't workout.

Maybe I choose poorly in my partnerships.

Maybe I don't know what the hell I'm doing when it comes to dating.

Culture dictates that we should have an idea of what we want by the time we are an adult. However, if you have made it this far in life, you know damn well that's not true. If anything, there's more confusion in midlife than there ever is as a young adult, due mostly in part by your life wisdom in the experiences you've already have. You realize by now, that life is complex and the answers do not flow easily. And yet, we still move through this space disallowing ourselves the ability to be kind in our understanding of this. If you can sit with yourself in silence and give yourself the grace and the respect of understanding that, not only do you not have the answers about life and dating, but that you should not have ever been expected to in the first place, is a huge step in healing.

If you have the cognition or the belief of self that you should have all the answers at any given time about any given issue in your life, you will be consistently confronted with a myriad of conflicted problems where you are expected to be able to take the helm with knowledge and grace. However, that rarely happens. Often, we find ourselves consistently cleaning up mess after mess after mess that we've made without any acknowledgement that maybe we should decide how to do things differently. If what we have been doing in the past, whether that is regarding dating and relationships or maybe our professional choices or how we manage our money for example, has not been working for us, we tend to not take the time necessary to readdress how we are metabolizing and manifesting those efforts.

The key word here is time.

You must take time for yourself to heal. You cannot be expected to motor through life at a high rate of speed and have all of the answers and the quick reflexes to make decisions on the fly. If that's what you've been doing, my recommendation for you right now, as you're reading this book, is to put a bookmark in, shut the book, and sit and take a few deep breaths.

Think about that.

Slow down.

Take your time.

Allow yourself time to consider what has happened.

Journal as a means to remind yourself.

Be honest with yourself.

Be honest and vulnerable in your journaling. There is no amount of therapy you can get that can replace you taking time for yourself to actually get to know who you are. It is funny. It is almost like you need to date yourself before you date someone else.

Get to know who you are.

Get to know your own red flags!

What kind of ass-hattery have you engaged in in the past?

If you can allow yourself to understand that we're all jerks at any given point in time it might be easier to assess this.

We've all screwed up.

No one is immune.

We've all treated people poorly at some point in our lives. Even the kindest, most empathetic, compassionate person you know has screwed up in a relationship with someone.

Understand this and you can learn to better allow yourself to accurately assess your own personal shortcomings.

It can be exhausting. I won't lie. It's hard work to sit with yourself and all your own personal bullshit to figure out what you've been doing. Don't you think you deserve the time to improve and grow? I think we can all agree that we have had these expectations for the people that we potentially partner with or people whom we have partnered with in the past to do the heavy emotional lifting in themselves and yet we often do not have the same expectation for ourselves.

Think of it more as an honor as opposed to a task or something to toil over that invokes a sense of shame. It doesn't have to be shameful to assess your shortcomings and to find areas of improvement as a means of bettering yourself in the future.

Ultimately, your purpose in doing this is not for someone else, but it's for you.

Only when you learn how to love yourself properly will you have the capacity to properly love someone else.

If you don't think you're worthy of love, how can you possibly justify a potential connection with a future partner that is worthy of love?

If you want a partner who is worthy of love, and you don't love yourself, then how can you properly give that person what they deserve?

If you can't take the time to heal and recover and get to know yourself after a breakup, what exactly is it you have to offer a new partnership?

It doesn't have to be painful, necessarily, as much as it is an uncomfortable point of growth. When you become comfortable with your discomfort is when you will really start to recognize the points of improvement.

Here are some examples of what to ask yourself.

In your past relationships, are you disrespectful?

In your past relationships, do you project upon your partners the blame that you see within yourself?

Do you find yourself feeling as though you are a victim in your past relationships?

Because you feel that you are a victim, do you feel entitled to disparage and or disrespect your partners?

These questions are not intended to shame you or make you feel bad about yourself, but instead to explain that when you project toxicity upon your partners, it is quite simply your projection of self.

In other words, people who have self-love and self-respect do not have it in them to disparage or disrespect their partners. It simply doesn't happen. People who feel that they are entitled to love and worthiness within themselves see their partners as equals, even if their partners are engaging in toxic behavior directed at them. It sounds very cliché, but it is true.

You simply cannot love someone else any more than you love yourself.

Until you learn to love yourself on your own terms, you will consistently meet partners and have connections with people that are like-minded and on that level. So, if you don't like who you are, then you're not going to have anything worthwhile to offer a person who has healed.

If you don't like who you are, you will consistently meet people who do not like themselves.

If you do not like who you are then you will only connect with people that you see yourself in.

If you elevate yourself through healing, by taking the time and talking to someone, such as a counselor, then the more healing work that you do on your journey will be mirrored in your potential partnerships.

When you actualize yourself by holding yourself accountable, being mindful and aware of your low-level actions in the past and then changing those patterns, you will see a vast improvement in the selection of potential partners you will meet in the future.

Rob is a 56-year-old tax attorney. When we first met, he came to me seeking advice on how to change his wife's mind about getting a divorce. I sat with him and listened to his story. He went on and on about how she spent too much money and never got a job and that her needs were never fulfilled.

Rob was extremely frustrated because he felt he had worked very hard to provide for their family and nothing he ever did seemed to satisfy her. Rob even went so far as to express that she had allowed herself to become overweight throughout their marriage and he admitted to me that he felt disgusted by how her body had changed. In his words, he felt it was unavoidable that he would cheat on her, which he admitted to on several occasions. Rob expressed to me that he didn't understand why his wife would want to leave him, because she's overweight and she'll never find anybody who makes as much money as he does. Rob also complained that she cried a lot and was always nagging him to spend more time with her. That initial meeting with Rob was him venting about how his wife had treated him unfairly. After about 30 minutes or so, Rob asked me what I thought about everything he had told me. As soon as I started to speak, Rob interrupted me to preface an additional point of the story, so I let him and paid attention to how he needed to control the narrative between us. I allowed him to speak for another 15 minutes.

Rob stopped. "You don't seem to have much to say for a counselor?"

I replied to Rob, "Often during these initial meetings, my clients tend to present in ways where they have felt unheard for a long time, and I want you to feel heard. Of course, I have plenty to say, but I want you to be able to express yourself freely without feeling any kind of judgment in our dynamic. Now that we only have 5 minutes left in our meeting do you have anything else you would like to add" I asked.

"I think we're going to need to have another meeting." he replied.

At our next meeting, Rob came in, sat down and smiled at me and said, "You're not going to believe what happened since we spoke last!" Rob appeared well dressed and in high spirits. He was smiling and gregarious. Rob then informed me that since our last meeting, he had met someone. He now expressed a desire to share with me how he couldn't believe he had actually met his soulmate. "Alma, she's beautiful! She's nothing like my wife. She appreciates what I do for a living and enjoys the time we share. She's never nagged me! I know it sounds crazy, but I think I might marry this woman after the divorce is final. I even told her that I wanted to!" I sat there and listened to Rob tell me all the wonderful features of the experience he had shared with this woman.

After about 20 minutes, I raised my hand and asked Rob if he would like my feedback. Rob stated "Oh I know what you're gonna say. You're going to tell me that it's too soon and that I need to take my time and date several people before I just make up my mind with one woman, right?" He laughed heartily.

I said, "Rob, in the short amount of time that you and I have worked together, I've spoken to you probably, maybe a total of 5 minutes. Do you see anything problematic with that?"

Rob paused and looked at me with concern "Well, you're the doc, Doc. Maybe you just need to tell me?" His tone was firm and respectful, but I could tell that his irritation with me was growing.

"Rob, I'm not here to judge you. I am not here to tell you what you're doing is right or wrong. That is not my purpose as a therapist. My purpose is to provide you with suitable feedback that you need to hear but not necessarily what you want to hear. If you will allow me the time you might find that what I have to say will surprise you. You may learn a few things about yourself that you're unaware of. What I would like to do right now is to provide you with a rational assessment of what I've seen going on with you."

Rob smiled and motioned for me to continue. I didn't explain to Rob that I suspected, based upon his behaviors with his wife, as well as his excitement over this newfound relationship, that he was starved for love and affection. Instead, I said I suspected, that as a small child, he was probably neglected as well. Rob's face dropped. I looked at him and said, "I can tell that what I'm saying to you is affecting you, based upon your expressions. First of all, we're all equal and worthy, Rob. Your desire for connection and love and affection is not something attributed to shame. I suspect, at some point in your life, you were made to feel that asking for affection made you less than or not worthy. I suspect wanting to be loved is something you have always felt the need to restrict or camouflage, as though it is something to be hidden. The truth is, wanting to be connected to someone else is a fundamental part of being a human being. We all need to feel a connection with others."

I went on to explain to Rob that I suspected that he was a workaholic as a means to cover up his need for connection, and he felt externally validated in being a very successful attorney who became wealthy because of all of his hard work. I went on to further hypothesize that many people who are financially successful workaholics, engage in that behavior because they do not feel like they are deserving or worthy of love in their own rights, so that they must create financial resources to build up their self-worth. I stopped speaking and looked at Rob. He turned towards the window to avoid eye contact. I then asked him if he felt what I was saying was resonating with how he felt.

Rob turned back to me with red eyes and stated, "I can't remember my father ever saying he loved me or that he was proud of me. My mother died when I was three. My father was married four times before he died when I was 45. None of those women ever wanted to be my mother. They only wanted my father's money. I don't think I know what love is to be honest with you." Rob then turned to look back out the window for a moment and then turned to me to say, "You know, I really expected that you were going to jump my ass for divorcing my wife and getting into this new relationship with Angela. I saw two therapists before you. Both times, I left angry because they made me feel worse about myself. You're the first person that gets it."

Our time was up and Rob scheduled for the following week. While we did make some headway initially, his habits did not effectively change for the long term as he broke up with Angela and preceded to engage in two back-to-back problematic relationships.

Fast forward two years later, Rob called and requested an urgent appointment. I conducted an immediate assessment to determine if he was in crisis, which he was not. I was able to schedule him within two days. When Rob arrived at my office, he appeared to be disheveled and as though he had not slept in many days. He sat down on the sofa in my office, placed his face in his hands and began to cry. I told Rob to take his time. We had practiced deep breathing techniques many times in our sessions and, without my prompting, Rob engaged himself in a deep breathing exercise.

"I'm here. Take your time. When you're ready, tell me what you're feeling."

Once Rob was able to compose himself enough to speak clearly, he looked at me and said, "Alma, everything that you've said to me over the past two years about my self-worth, I felt was total bullshit. I really thought you were a quack as far as telling me that I was worth something, but the funny thing is I did not think that consciously, but it was what I felt about you and about our relationship here. I was willing to keep coming to you for help even though I felt that you didn't have any clue about what you were talking about with my self-worth. Three days ago, Melanie left. The sad thing is that when she left me, I didn't care. She told me she had met someone and was leaving me, and I didn't feel anything, Alma. She's gorgeous and smart and funny and talented and she's got a wonderful job that she's great at. Yet, I didn't see her. What I did see was myself and I treated her accordingly. When she left the other night, Alma, I realized what you were talking about. The whole time I dated her and the whole time that I dated Alicia and the whole time that I dated Angela, I didn't see them for who they were, I only saw myself. And I have, my whole life, thought that I was just a worthless piece of shit because that's what my father taught me about myself. My father hated himself too, of course I, as an extension of him, had to be equally worthless. So obviously, for me, if somebody wants to spend time with me, then they must be a piece of shit too and so I treated them like they were pieces of shit, because I see myself as a piece of shit. Now that I look at all of these people I've hurt, I realize that I really am a piece of shit because of how I've treated them. I don't deserve to be with these kinds of women. I don't deserve to be cared for and loved. Hell, my wife always told me how much she loved me, but I never believed her. I never believed that she was with me because she genuinely cared about me, I thought she was with me because she was a beautiful woman and, if I didn't make a lot of money, she would leave me for somebody better than me. It was always a competition, Alma! I was always in competition with some phantom guy who could sneak in and take my partner away from me at any given time because I am a piece of shit! I don't deserve to be loved! I don't deserve to be with beautiful people who love me! When Melanie left, I thought about everything that you've said to me. And I started thinking maybe I am the problem."

After Rob and I engaged in another deep breathing exercise, I looked at him sternly and said, "Are you ready now?" Rob nodded his head in a yes fashion and then preceded to cry.

"Rob, why would I lie to you? Think about this logically. Why would I go to school and write all those papers and kick my own ass for years, struggling, taking on student loan debt only to sit here in front of you and feed your head full of lies? Why would I say something to you that was untrue?"

Rob looked at me and said, "You wouldn't. You haven't. I just don't know how to process what you're telling me."

I smiled at Rob and said "Rob, I think that's the first honest response you've ever given me in two years. It's also the healthiest thing you've ever said, in my opinion, at least to me, anyway."

Rob appeared confused.

"Let me explain something to you," I replied. "Don't you think it's easier to accept the fact that you are deserving of love, than it is to accept the fact that you're a piece of shit like your father told you? Let's talk a little bit about your father's motivations in telling you that and making you feel that way. See, most of us grow up with the assumption that our caregivers treat us with the kind of love and concern that we deserve. It's an implication that the people who are supposed to take care of us should give us accurate feedback. So, when our caregivers engage in manipulative, toxic, harmful, abusive, and otherwise negative and adverse ways, we automatically assume it is accurate because they are our caregivers. I am merely here, sitting in front of you as a therapist and sharing with you that is not necessarily true. Think about it this way, Rob. Don't you think it is easier to reframe that belief set about your father being accurate in his description of you? Why is it so hard to believe that your father was full of shit? Because to me, it seems like he was a broken man who was hurt, probably by his parents. Don't you think it's possible that your father just did not know how to love you and, as a result, he felt shame and so it was easier for him to project his feelings about himself onto you? Just because he told you those awful things does not make it true. Just because your father said that you are a worthless piece of shit doesn't mean that it's true. Don't you think it's possible that he did that to you because he was hurting himself? Your father was cruel. Your father was abusive. Your father created this cognition in yourself to believe that you did not deserve love because of the way he treated you. That absolutely shifted the development of your personality into the mindset that it exists in today. Your father taught you how to hate yourself because he hated himself. The only thing that you can now do is relearn how you feel about yourself. And once you break it down in very elemental terms like that, it is actually quite simple and it's actually quite easy when you allow yourself to love and be loved in a healthy and appropriate fashion. Eventually, throughout a therapeutic relationship, you may actually be able to forgive your father for how he treated you."

Rob was staring at me with wide eyes. "I get what you're saying, Alma, and it's all true. I am ready. I do want to change. But how do I clean up all this shit? Look at all the people I've hurt! I don't even know how to begin to start coming back from all of the pain I've caused. I am so incredibly ashamed of myself. My wife put up with my shit for so long, I am surprised she lasted as long as she did. These last three women after my divorce did not deserve any of the shit I put them through, either. Angela quit her job to move in with me at my condo and what did I do to repay her? I cheated on her with Alicia. When Angela found out, she left me, so Alicia moved in. Alicia wanted to start a baking business and I rented out the space for her to have her start up. I felt that by giving her things, that would make her love me. I could tell Alicia didn't respect me, even though I had supported her business. She still has that baking company and she paid me back the money for the investment. Then she broke up with me. At the time, I thought there was no reason for the breakup, but now I know she was not being loved the way she wanted to be loved. Of course, you know I was feeling sorry for myself when she left me. That's when

I met Melanie on a work trip. Man, Melanie really kicked my ass! We met and sparks flew. She had just gotten out of a marriage. We had sexual chemistry and intellectual chemistry and I immediately wanted to wife her up too. She left me because she met someone else. I know I should have been hurt, but honestly, I was just numb. I'm tired, Alma. I don't know what to do and I'm tired of hiding how I feel. I'm ready to listen to you. I trust you and I know that you know what you are talking about. I am sorry I didn't believe you before. It was just easier for me to invalidate your knowledge and willfulness to help me, than it was for me to actually believe what you were saying."

Rob then smiled at me and said, "You know the funny thing, Alma? I believe you. I actually do believe that I'm worthy of being loved. I just do not know where to start or what to do now. I want to be happy and connected with someone. I do not trust myself to do that though. I don't trust myself to make good decisions. I end up hurting everybody that I interact with. I lie constantly in relationships. I don't know how to tell the truth because, for some reason, the truth is either boring or inconvenient. At worst, the truth will end things that I am trying to manipulate for my own will. I don't want to be that person anymore. I just don't know how to stop."

Rob and I continued to work together for about three more months. He agreed to take some time to himself and to not date or have casual encounters with women. We visited weekly and Rob would bring in his journal entries as homework. He made great strides in recognizing how his childhood affected his decision-making. He filed paperwork with his partnership to retire and took some savings to purchase a small sailboat. Rob had been a sailor all his life and it was something that his father had taught him to do as a young boy. However, due to his workaholic mentality, Rob had not engaged in sailing in several years. After several weeks of sailing, Rob came in for his appointment and told me he had been spending time with another woman that he was growing very fond of.

"She's nothing like all of the women I have dated in the past, Alma. If I'm being completely honest, when I first met her, I found nothing about her appealing at all. She's not what I'm attracted to physically. However, I realized that in the past, I was driven by my sexual desire and allowing that to make decisions for me. I legitimately did not expect to grow into this friendship with this woman. She taught the sailing class I was in. She has a beautiful boat and has been sailing all her life. I don't know if this connection with this woman is going to be something that will turn into a romantic relationship, but I can honestly say that I'm not trying to label it and that feels good. I like her. I respect her. She is witty and, now that I've grown into this friendship with her, there is a beauty and a depth about her that rivets me to my core. I just wanted you to know that and that I'm being mindful and fair and honest with her. All of this is different. It's not rushed. In all my life, I have never been in a relationship with a woman where I felt like she was my friend first. This woman is my friend, Alma, and whether or not we end up in a romantic relationship is no concern for me because I know I have her friendship."

After a few more sessions, I didn't see Rob again for three years. Out of the blue, he calls me up to say, "Alma, I never thanked you. I just want you to know that Julie and I got married. If you ever want to stop by the pier, we own the school and I'm now a sailing instructor. I want you to know that I wrote letters to all the women. A few of them got really angry and called me and cussed me out." He laughed. "I know. I deserved it! But it felt good to reach out and let them know that I was sorry for everything. Melanie, strangely enough, wanted to see me, and I had to tell her that I was in a committed relationship and that I wished her well. She hung up on me and I never heard back from her. Alicia is married.

She was very sweet and told me she was very happy that I was happy. I'm sure that, if I knew then what I know now, Alicia and I could have had a life together, but it makes me happy to know she's found someone to share her life with. So, thank you, Alma. If you ever want free sailing lessons, just let me know!"

You must take the time to heal.

You have to take the initiative to work with a therapist who can help you disentangle your inaccurate cognitions and beliefs about yourself. Otherwise, you keep making the same decisions as Rob did. Just like Rob, you are worthy.

You deserve love.

You deserve happiness.

CHAPTER SIX

Toxic behaviors: Lynn's story

We have all been there. We have all been hurt, which often results in our own behaviors that are manipulative, dysfunctional, and overall, just toxic in general.

It sucks to get your feelings hurt in relationships. Furthermore, when we have consistently been in relationships with other people where our feelings are discounted and / or not even appreciated or respected, it can almost feel as though it is necessary to behave in a manipulative fashion in future relationships to prevent that feeling from occurring again. No one wants to be hurt. The truth of the matter is we all, as human beings, share a desire to connect with others. We all need community. We all need friends and people that we care about to love us and support us.

As we move through life, those connections can become incredibly confusing and convoluted when there is toxic behavior involved. Our belief system regarding what healthy relationships should look like becomes very murky when we experience nothing but pain and regret. At the end of the day, we all just want to trust ourselves enough to make good decisions when it comes to choosing a partner. When we do not trust ourselves, we have a tendency to lean into behaviors that sabotage our happiness in the long run. Hell, we may even feel like we must treat other people poorly as a means to gain an advantage in a relationship. Ghosting, lying and other manipulative tactics that are routinely employed in relationship building, can oftentimes feel like a toolbox for safety. It is, on the shorthand of things, because when we create a dynamic where we position ourselves in the interaction with other people in a position of disconnect and or lack of feeling or love for that person, we can feel somewhat empowered. However, there is lack of depth and lack of connection when we are not capable or do not allow ourselves to be vulnerable in those interactions. The only way two people can genuinely and authentically connect, is when both people enter the connection with an open-mindedness that is willful and honest.

Unfortunately, during middle age, after having left long-term relationships, these relationships have created a cognition within us to believe that other people simply cannot be trusted and the only way that we can cultivate some form of connection is to be manipulative. However, it does not have to be that way. I often express to my clients a desire to inspire them. I feel like it is my purpose in this life to encourage other people to grow into their highest self. It is extremely validating for me, not just as a therapist, but as a human being, to be someone who can be a demonstration of what it looks like to achieve your purpose in life. Of course, I have engaged in toxic behaviors in my own personal interactions. It is not something I'm proud of, but to reiterate the fact that in order to attain that purpose and to attain that highest version of the self, you must be authentic, which is what I'm trying to do right now.

Being toxic can feel incredibly powerful.

Manipulating someone you have feelings for can give you a perceived feeling of advantage in the situation because it makes you feel safe, albeit in a dysfunctional fashion. When you wait to return a phone call or wait a day or two to return that text because you do not want the other person to perceive you as having any kind of urgency in your desire to connect with them, can give you a feeling of advantage. I think it is safe to say that in midlife, especially after leaving long term relationships, we have all experienced what it feels like to interact with someone who does not play games. It can feel very daunting to have that kind of attention and interaction. It feels like pressure because, when someone does not reserve themselves and their interaction is open, they are vulnerable with their feelings and a desire to connect and / or commit to you can make you feel like you're in a pressure cooker. Particularly, when you do not necessarily share the same feelings, it can feel quite off-putting to have that level of attention from someone else. Therefore, because of those experiences as well, we do not want a potential partner to perceive us as overly eager and therefore, lose interest in us. So, we play the waiting game. We interact and give our attention fully and experience the elation of a connected face-to-face conversation or a two-hour phone call. On the other end of that, we might have feelings of regret that we allowed ourselves to have that type of vulnerability, so as a means to lessen the perception of availability, we might step away for several days and not interact with that person.

While this behavior is not necessarily toxic, it's important to understand the underpinnings as to why we behave this way to begin with. The work I do substantiates the fact that most people do not take the time to sit with their feelings long enough so they are able to articulate what they want to do moving forward with a particular person. Many times, we get so burdened with the obligations of life; whether it's children, profession, education, hobbies and recreation, etc., we tend to overburden ourselves to the point where we simply do not sit and think and contemplate what we feel.

Feeling hurts.

Feeling our feelings can be terribly uncomfortable, particularly when they are feelings that we feel disempowered by.

When we express an interest in someone else in the dating game, we open ourselves up for the potential pain to occur that we have already experienced and that we possess no desire to return to.

Nobody wants to be hurt. So, we play games. At the end of the day, we may even subconsciously make a choice to hurt someone else to protect ourselves and that, in and of itself, is the definition of toxicity.

I can't help but sit back and think about Lynn, a 49-year-old, three-time divorced mother with two adult sons. Lynn initially came to me requesting help with insomnia. She arrived 10 minutes late to our first appointment. A tall, shapely, white female with long flowing red hair, she flashed me a brilliant, charismatic smile as she apologized for her tardiness. I pointed towards the sofa and asked her to please take a seat and offered her a glass of water, which she declined as she withdrew a bottle of Diet Coke from her Michael Kors handbag. She took a moment to position herself comfortably on the sofa in my office. She reached across and repositioned the cushions and tossed the quilt haphazardly to the opposite end of the sofa in a crumpled pile. I sat across from her in my office chair and sipped on my ice water as I asked her what she would like to talk about. Before I could finish my sentence, Lynn began to wave her hands and to speak in an urgent fashion about how horrible her boss is.

"He's an incredible asshole! You wouldn't believe it. You cannot possibly imagine what an incredible narcissist this man is!" She laughed loudly, as though she were intentional with her comedy. "Alma, he actually reminds me of my ex-husband!"

"What's going on in your situation at work with him?" I asked.

"Well, for one, he wrote me up for being tardy to work, but didn't even give me a chance to explain to him that I had to take care of something for my son."

As per normal, I sat and listened to Lynn disclose the problems with her work, as she detailed her perception of being misaligned and maltreated in her work environment. She expressed hostility, resentment, sadness, and vacillated rapidly between the variables of these emotions, to the point she became tearful when describing how she really felt about her boss.

"He's married and he hits on me all the time, Alma!"

"What do you mean?" I asked her.

"OK, so I'm sure you figured it out by now, but we're sleeping together. I can't believe that he would write me up for being late after I told him I loved him and that I am in love with him. How can he do that to me? I mean, I know I'm an employee, but don't you think that if we're having sex, that he'd ignore the fact I'm coming into work late?" She continued to detail how their affair began.

As her tone and cadence started to slow down, she began to quietly cry. "What is it that you're feeling right now?" I inquired.

She took a few moments to compose herself, followed by a couple of deep breaths which I encouraged her to take her time with.

"I just feel used. I feel like I am never going to be enough. I feel like I am never going to find somebody who wants to be with me for me. I feel like I must do something in order to get someone else to do something for me. I am so lonely all the time. He gets to have sex with me at work and then he goes home to his wife that he shares his bed with. I have sex with him at work and I go home to my messy apartment and sit and binge watch Netflix by myself. I get angry sometimes, you know, Alma. It's just not fucking fair! You know, I created a fake Facebook account, and I friended his wife? I look at her page and I can see all of his family photos and how happy he looks with her. I know what you're going to say! I know that I'm asking for trouble. Why can't I be happy? Why can't I have the life that he gives her? Why am I not enough?"

She began to sob and with wiping her eyes she peeled away her false eyelashes with a chuckle.

"Everything about me is fake." She pointed to her breasts, "At least these are mine!" She laughed through her tears. "I got married right out of high school. God, Alma, you should have seen me. I was so fucking hot! I could have had anybody! What the fuck was I thinking getting married at 18? I look back at pictures of myself and I could have done anything. But I married Mark because he told me he loved me. So, what happened? He got me pregnant. We lasted for two years and during those two years, while I was staying at home in our single wide trailer taking care of our son, he was out cheating on me with my best friend and another lady from his work. Do you know what really pisses me off? He's still married to that lady from work. After we got divorced they got married and that was 25 years ago! Do you know how bad that makes me feel? Do you know that when we got divorced, he came to our hearing with her? She was pregnant then. They have had three kids since then, Alma! Why the fuck wasn't I enough! Those were awful days. I was crazy with jealousy. After he left, I used to drive by their house. I even egged her car once. She called me up and cussed me out and I denied it, of course. This was before Ring cameras or any kind of security. I'd never do that shit now!"

She stopped talking suddenly, leaned back into the sofa, glanced around the office and then looked at me directly and asked, "Why can't I be happy?"

I took a moment and considered her question and responded to her, "I know it's going to sound cliché, but seriously, Lynn, I think the reason that you are consistently finding yourself wrapped up in these same situations over and over again, has nothing to do with these people, but everything to do with how you see yourself. If you are consistently interacting with low level people who treat you poorly, then perhaps, instead of looking at them, maybe look at yourself for a moment."

She cut me off. "I knew you were going to say that. I knew you were going to say it was all my fault! But you are right. I know

I am a piece of shit. Hell, that is what my second husband told me. We were on our honeymoon, and I got food poisoning. Can you fucking believe that?! I got food poisoning at my own reception. Hell, everybody was sick. His parents were the ones that paid for that caterer, not me. I was throwing up and he was still wanting me to have sex with him. He told me I was a piece of shit and that I was a disappointment as a wife. This was on our wedding night, Alma!"

I allowed her to finish her sentence and then I interjected with, "I never said you were a piece of shit. Also, I want to remind you, that in this therapeutic engagement, please remember that if we're going to be able to work together, we need to hold space for each other's boundaries. I need you to understand it is important we build trust together and that we both respect that trust. What I mean by that, Lynn, is that it is not helpful if you sit there and become defensive with me because of something you assume I am saying. When I expressed to you that you need to look inward and that you need to do the introspection into yourself, is exactly what I mean. It is not intended to blame you or make you feel less than. It is an open invitation for you to consider the choices you have been making, as well as perhaps some questionable boundaries. I think you have been getting involved in these situations simply because you just don't know any better. I do not think you've had the opportunity to really evaluate who you are, where the problem lies, and how to fix it. There is no judgement to be had in that process. Keep in mind, that in the process, if you are doing it correctly and you're being authentic, you will find behaviors, mannerisms, etc. that you are engaging in that are problematic. It is not intended to make you feel bad about yourself, but more to help you grow into a healthier version of yourself who makes better life choices and chooses better partners. But you must start with yourself, because when we choose partners, we tend to choose people that we mirror. So, if you don't think that you're worth anything, you're going to be selecting partners who mirror that about you."

Lynn avoided my eyes and appeared to be interested in the artwork on my wall. "I don't know about that. I feel like you're trying to tell me that all of this is my fault."

"Well Lynn, I wouldn't word it that way because that's judgmental language. What I would say, is that you possess the authority and the ability to decide on how you are going to move forward in your life and how you are going to change your behaviors for the better, based upon the acknowledgment of problematic behaviors and choices in your past. Blame is irrelevant. Granted, yes, you could say that it is 'your fault' that you made poor choices, but that comes from a place of low sense of self-worth. The point I am trying to make with you, as I would make with any client, is that instead of engaging that shame response that makes you feel bad about yourself, instead, look at it from a perspective of challenging yourself in a space of love for yourself."

She rolled her eyes at me and then flashed me a brilliant smile. "I know what you're trying to do."

"And what is that?" I smiled back at her.

"You're trying to use that psychological bullshit to get me to see how bad I am fucked up in my head so that I can see how much I fucked up my own life. Am I right?"

"Yes. Although I wouldn't phrase it that way."

She sneered. "See! This is why I can't find a decent husband or a decent therapist!" She started to collect her things as if she were getting ready to leave.

"I can't stop you, Lynn. I am not going to try to stop you. I will say that I do not think you've ever had the opportunity to really figure out what it is you deserve in life. I think you are hurting deeply. I think you want and I think you deserve to be loved unconditionally. I think you are so desperate for it, that you're willing to create scenarios that are unhealthy, toxic and dysfunctional in order to get your needs met. I think you are ashamed of some of the behaviors that you've had to engage in, in order to get people to connect with you. I do not think you're a bad person. Quite the opposite. I think you do what you do because you feel it's what you have to do in order to get your needs met. I think you have been in scenarios your entire life, where you have felt the need to think and feel a certain way that simply has not served you well. If you do not know how to do something because you've never learned how to do it, then how can you hold yourself accountable in a place of blame and judgment?"

She slid her handbag across the side of the sofa and crossed her arms. "What are you talking about?"

"First of all, I'm not your enemy. I cannot speak for other therapists, but I can tell you right now, the way you are acting toward me, I find a bit off-putting. However, I will challenge you in your behavior. I think you need a little bit of pushback because that's what your normal go to is. I think you are only comfortable in chaos. I think you intentionally target and / or project your hostilities onto others just to see how much they are willing to engage you. I think that is where you get a sense of worthiness, and external validation by challenging other people in manipulative ways to see how much they actually care about you. I think that is your normal go to because you don't know any better. Your attempt to use these tactics with me will simply cause us to have a little bit of a longer time building rapport or you'll just get pissed off at me and try to find another therapist. I can tell you this much, that while I may not tell you what you want to hear, I will always tell you what you need to hear, Lynn. I say this to all my clients. I don't think you know what you're doing and I'm here to help you. I am not here to judge you. I am not here to make you feel ashamed of yourself. But I will tell you that I do think you are making some very poor choices. The fact that I think you are the causation for all of your unhappiness is irrelevant. In fact, it gives you an enormous amount of power, don't you think? You can only control two things, anyway. Those are your actions and your reactions to other people. You can't control other people and how they feel toward you. You can't control how other people treat you. However, you can do the work and figure out what it is you're doing that is sabotaging your ability to find happiness. You can do this without self-blame and low self-worth. You can do this by sitting with all your decisions and acknowledging them without being self-deprecating. The thing is, Lynn, you just don't value yourself enough. That's not a judgment, but an observation. It comes from a long withstanding cognition of how you see yourself. I'm certain that it started when you were a child. Someone made you think you were not worth enough at some point in your early development. I don't know who that person or people were, but I know it had a deeply rooted effect on how your personality developed into this belief about how you see yourself. As a cognitive behavioral therapist, I can tell you right now, without hesitation, that there is an incredible amount of power to be had in looking at what you are doing in your life versus trying to control the actions of others. It must be terribly exhausting to sit around on your computer or your phone at night, scrolling through the Facebook profile of the wife of the man you're sleeping with. That must make you feel horrendous. I can only imagine why you're doing it, but if you don't sit and tell me what you're genuinely feeling when you're doing it, then there's a limitation on how I can help you."

Lynn took a deep breath, "So what do you think I should do? Are you telling me I should delete her as a friend on Facebook?"

"Lynn, I think it's much deeper than that. I think when you assess the ways in which you invest your emotional energy and you become more willful in utilizing your emotional strength in ways that are more productive and healthier, I think you'll come to the conclusion on what you need to do. We can continue to work on this and to isolate the behaviors that you've engaged in, and we can also discuss why those behaviors are problematic. When you drive by the girlfriend's house of your ex-husband and egg her car, or when you choose to create fake Facebook profiles to keep tabs on the person you're sleeping with, through these actions you are eroding your self-worth because you are allowing your emotional energy to be invested in areas that are simply beneath you. You just don't believe they're beneath you or you haven't really given it any thought. The question remains, and it's a starting point for you, Lynn, how much is your time worth? Doesn't it tire you out feeling that you're not enough? Honestly, I think you're used to it because I think you feel like that's all you're worth."

"Well, you might have a point. I guess, in a way, I can see what you're talking about. I just feel like it is all I can do sometimes. Do you know what I mean?"

"Absolutely. that's a great starting point for us."

"Alma, do you think there's any hope for me? Is all of this therapy going to help me find love that's going to last forever?"

"Yes, IF you do the work. It absolutely will. However, I don't think you realize the kind of love it is that you need. You have to learn how to love yourself. Until that happens, you will continue to function in toxic ways and will continue to manipulate potential partners because you simply don't love yourself enough to not do so. When you learn how to love yourself, you will start to engage in healthier and more respectful ways of expending your emotional energy. When you love yourself and respect yourself, you won't feel compelled to egg someone's car and you won't create fake social media profiles as a means of snooping on someone else's life. When you love yourself, you will realize that you are deserving of your own partnership, where that person is invested in you and you alone. This results in negating the need to check in on someone else altogether. It must start with you. This fulfillment that you seek resides inside you and no one else. You have to be willful in making the choice today that you simply do not want to continue feeling the way you do. The first step is to believe that you deserve to make these changes. Lynn, do you think that you deserve to find this love that you seek?"

"Jesus, I honestly don't know. When you ask me that question, I want to say yes, but I really don't know. I don't see myself that way. I don't see myself as someone who is deserving of anything."

I smiled at her and looked at the clock. "Let's get you scheduled for next week OK? For now, I want you to pick up a journal and start writing down your thoughts. There is no rhyme or reason to this, but just write down how you're feeling at any given moment of the day. The more authentic you are about how you genuinely feel at any given moment and you chronicle that in a journal, it is directly related to the speed with which you will start to grow, learn and heal. It might feel weird and uncomfortable at first, putting pen to paper and writing down your deepest held feelings. If you're feeling sad, write that down. If you are feeling angry, write that down and write down why you're feeling angry. It's important to write down why you are feeling angry, especially when you feel ashamed that you're angry. Do as much as you can before our next visit. We can sit down, and we can talk about as much as you're comfortable with. How does that sound?"

She grabbed her handbag and tossed her empty Diet Coke bottle into my wastebin. "We'll see."

Three days later, Lynn called me crying, requesting an urgent meeting in a voicemail message I did not receive until after the end of my business day. I returned her phone call and she answered breathlessly "Finally! I've been waiting for you to call me back all day!"

"Lynn, please understand that I have other clients that I must see. Also, know this, I would never intentionally avoid you. I am simply busy working with other clients and taking time for myself as well. This is the normal time that I answer these kinds of calls. I don't have any openings before your prescheduled appointment. Are you safe?", I inquired.

"Safe?" She responded in an almost astonished tone. "I guess so, Alma. I am not going to blow my brains out, if that's what you're asking. I am just upset because I had to quit my job. He was going to fire me anyway."

"Well, that's definitely something we can talk about at your appointment."

"Fine," she said and hung up on me.

When Lynn arrived for her second appointment with me, she presented in athletic gear and her hair in a messy pony-tail. This time she was only 5 minutes late. I ushered her in and she readily took her space on the sofa. "I'm sorry I was rude to you the other day. I know you are just trying to help me, and I know you're busy. It is just that every therapist I've ever talked to gets really shitty with me at this point. You've actually been very nice, and I appreciate it."

I thanked her and offered her something to drink, which she declined. "Tell me what happened with the job".

"Well, I knew he was going to fire me, so I had to go. So here I am, once again, living on leftover savings and wondering what I'm going to do for a paycheck."

I repeated my question. "Do you want to tell me what happened with the job?"

"Alma, it was unavoidable. It was going to happen eventually. So, I went to my boss's house. He wasn't home but she was. She seemed to know who I am because of the way she looked at me and how she treated me when she answered the door."

"Why did you go to your boss's house?" I already knew the answer to this question, but I needed her to express it in her terms.

"He broke up with me. He said that he did not want to break up his family by having sex with me. Alma, you don't understand what it's like. He told me that he loved me. He told me that he wanted to marry me one day! Hell, I believed him! Then, all of a sudden, he pulls me into his office and says he's going to take me to lunch. Alma, I was actually excited! He'd never done that before! He usually hid everything that we were doing together. I thought maybe we were making a turn! Instead, he took me to a busy restaurant so that he could tell me he wasn't going to sleep with me anymore and he was hoping that, being out in public, I wouldn't make a scene! He was wrong about that! I chewed his ass out up one side and down the other! I told him what a piece of shit he was for cheating on his wife. He just sat there and stared at me. He told me I needed to calm down and that just made it worse. I lied to him and told him I quit my job and then I'm going home and that he's never going to have to worry about seeing me again. I didn't go home though, Alma. I went to his house. I knew that it was my only chance to get to her before he could."

"How did that workout for you, Lynn?"

"Apparently, he had already told her about me. Because when she answered the door, she said that I was not welcome there and to never come back. I told her some nasty things, Alma. Can you believe I told that woman that if she would have taken better care of her husband that he would not have come to me for sex? Now, why the fuck would I say something like that to her? I'm so fucking angry right now. I'm so hurt. I'm so jealous of her!"

"Tell me what happened next, Lynn."

"Well, she told me that if I showed up at her doorstep again, she was going to call the police. She told me to stay away from her husband and she said I was the ugliest cunt that he had ever cheated with."

Lynn and I shared an extended moment of silence. I scooted my rolling office chair a little bit closer into her personal space and extended my hand. She looked at me quizzically. I nodded for her to give me her hand. She was a bit reserved at first, but then extended her hand to me. I took her hand in both of mine and said, "Lynn, when you walked away from confronting his wife, what did you think about yourself in that moment?" She dropped her head, and I could see tears streaming down her face.

"I felt dirty. I felt used. I feel worthless right now, just telling you that story."

"Lynn, do you realize that just because you feel worthless, doesn't mean it's true?"

"Yeah, but I'm the one who went to her house. I'm the one who fucked her husband. That makes me the bad guy. That makes me a piece of shit. That makes me worthless."

I argued with her "No, Lynn, it doesn't and here's why. You went to her house because you were in pain. You went to her house because you felt disempowered and out of control over a situation that you simply did not want to take place. You fucked her husband because you're lonely and you want love desperately. You allowed yourself to become involved with a married man because you don't feel like you're worth anything better. You allow other people to see you and use you on the terms that you see yourself. He recognized your low sense of worth and for whatever reason decided to engage upon this sexual relationship with you out of his own dysfunctional needs for affection and sexual gratification. Lynn, you're not a bad guy. True, you have engaged in some toxic behaviors. Engaging in a behavior is only representative of your sense of self-worth, not of your actual value."

"Explain that to me some more, Alma, because I don't understand what you mean."

"I mean, that what you see about yourself is inaccurate. You believe that you are the bad guy. The truth is, you were never given the tools to stand up and enforce boundaries and to see your actual worth in a healthy way, because you have never experienced it. That is a fair and accurate representation of who and what you are. Don't you think it makes more sense to recognize that when you were little, you simply were not taught to love yourself in a healthy way? When you honestly rationalize the logic in your statement, it absolutely holds no water, Lynn."

She was focused on my every breath as I continued to speak. " Think about it. Take all of the nasty shit and toxic behaviors that you have ever engaged in with regards to your romantic relationships in your entire life and take them off the table. Look at yourself physically in a mirror and I want you to explain to me what it is about you that makes you so unworthy. Don't get wrapped up in your toxic behavior. We will address that at an appropriate time but, for now, we are going to set aside all of the behaviors that you have engaged upon and not address those as a barometer of your worth. Forget about all the shitty things you have ever done and suspend your disbelief and play along. Just humor me, as your therapist. What is it about yourself that makes you so unworthy?"

"I Don't know. I honestly don't. I've just always felt this way."

"OK, let's do this then. Can you think back to when you were a child, when you were proud of yourself or when someone expressed pride in your behavior or told you that you are loved and appreciated and valued?"

"Oh, that's easy" She stated. "My grandmother was always my biggest cheerleader. I loved spending time with her. When my parents got divorced, my mother would never let me see her because she hated my father so much, and since that was his mother, she wanted to punish my dad any way she could. My dad could be a total asshole. But his mother was a beautiful person. She died shortly after me and my mom moved out of state, after my parents got divorced. I did not even get to go to her funeral. I was 8. I still miss her and it's been over 40 years."

"Lynn, what do you think your grandmother would say to you about how you feel about yourself today?" She seemed puzzled by the question.

"I don't know. She would probably argue with me and tell me I was wrong for feeling bad about myself."

"Go on," I encouraged her to continue.

She took a deep breath and sighed, "She loved me so much, Alma. To see me like this now would make her heart sick. She thought I was the perfect, sweetest, kindest child. I think it would make her very sad to see me like this. No one ever loved me the way she did and I lost her."

"But did you really?" I carefully inquired. "I don't know. Maybe I'm more of a modern-day hippie when it comes to my therapeutic approach" I smiled at her. "I think that the love of a grandmother is an incredibly special thing and even though they pass away, the love they have for us, we carry deep within us for the rest of our lives. I honestly believe you have a tool here that you have not been using. I think the concept of your grandmother's love and how she made you feel about yourself as a small child, has an incredible amount of power in helping you to evolve and grow into the best version of yourself today, as a grown woman. Think about it, Lynn. Do you think, hypothetically, if your grandmother were still alive today and you had the opportunity to have a very close relationship with her, that you would feel this way about yourself?"

"Absolutely not. She would never allow it. She would not tolerate seeing me treat myself the way I do."

"This might feel a little bit argumentative," I interjected, "but don't you feel it's a little bit disregarding of the impact of her influence on you by ignoring what she did to impact your life in such a positive fashion? Let me take it one step further, Lynn. Imagine that you passed away and left this earthly plane, but your spirit was still walking around, and you are observing how the people you left behind are living their lives. Wouldn't you be a little bit upset to see the people you gave all that love to, treat themselves badly? Don't you think that…." I paused to collect my thoughts. "I don't know. It might sound a little bit silly, but wouldn't you feel a little bit hurt that the people you loved so much while you were still alive, forgot that? I guess what I'm trying to say to you is, there's a way you can honor your grandmother by actualizing your self love because she believed in you, that you can learn to believe in yourself and have worth as well."

Lynn smiled. "Wow. I never really thought about it that way. You know, sometimes I dream about her. I dream about her and then, when I wake up, I'm so sad that I have to go on living without her. It feels like an elephant on my chest, Alma. She died over 40 years ago, for crying out loud. I should be over it by now."

"Love does not have an expiration date, my dear. Just because your grandmother passed away, doesn't mean you have to stop allowing her to love you. In fact, I would encourage you to think back on how deeply rooted her love was for you when she was here on this earth. Her love can be the starting point for you actualizing your love for yourself. It can also provide you with the ability to better define what love looks like in a healthy way. It sounds like she was the only healthy love you ever experienced. From a therapeutic standpoint, it makes sense that you behave the way you do in relationships with other people. You just don't know any better. You were never given the opportunity to grow into the healthiest version of yourself. That is, until now."

"I like your style, Alma." She volunteered. "I guess I never felt like I had the permission. In a lot of ways, I tried to forget about my grandmother because my mother resented her so much when she was alive. My mother tried to love me, but she had her own problems. I think she was jealous of my relationship with my grandmother in a lot of ways. I think that's why my mother wouldn't let me go to the funeral. You know, it's funny, thinking back all those years ago, I can still remember how all of those events made me feel. Now that I'm older I think I have a better understanding about why my mother behaved the way that she did. I don't think that she considered the impact of her behavior. Hell, I know I've screwed my kids up in a lot of ways. My dad didn't treat my mom well. I can't be mad at her for how she felt 40 years ago towards her mother-in-law. But damn, if it didn't break my heart when my grandma died. Later on, I didn't feel like I could even talk about her with my mom and then I just tried to forget her altogether." Lynn began to weep. I reached over to my desk to grab the tissues and handed the box to her.

"Take your time, Lynn. Feel this. When you're ready, tell me what it is you're feeling."

After several minutes and several used tissues, Lynn took a deep breath. "God!" she gasped while holding her abdomen tightly " I fucking miss her so much! I miss her smell. I miss how fucking safe she made me feel. My parents would always drop me off with her when they would fight or when they would go fuck somewhere for the weekend, when my dad had to make it up to my mom for cheating on her again. I didn't care! I felt most at home with my grandmother anyway. Jesus Christ, Alma! I just remembered how excited I was when I heard that my parents were getting divorced. My initial response to that was the hope I would get to go live with my grandmother!"

I surveyed the clock and realized that we had gone 10 minutes over our session time. We scheduled our next visit and this time she asked for a hug upon her departure, which I readily obliged.

Over the next six months, I met with Lynn regularly. Her sense of self-worth, while slow at first, graduated into a healthy version of a woman who allowed herself the grace and understanding of her own behaviors and how they have been sabotaging her happiness throughout her entire adult life. She engaged in frank and open discussions with her adult sons about how her behavior had affected them, by creating adverse conditions. Over our sessions, she expressed a willful intent to address her shortcomings with love and understanding for herself, as well as intention on changing her behavior for the better. Her sleep patterns improved remarkably. She found a new job and teased herself a bit about not wanting to sleep with her boss this time. She was jovial and happy in her newfound single life. She cut off all ties with her past relationships and decided she wanted to go back to school to become a paralegal. She stayed busy and, after 8 months of therapy, chose to not schedule anymore visits.

After another year and a half, I received a phone call from Lynn requesting to meet. She arrived at my office appearing healthy and happy. She had expressed she had been dating someone but soon discovered that he was manipulative and treating her disrespectfully.

"Alma, you'd be so proud of me. In the past, I would have tolerated it. I would have allowed him to continue to treat me the way he was starting to treat me. I recognized the red flags and I challenged him by enforcing a boundary, just like you taught me. He didn't like that and he started name-calling. He said I was a bitch who thought I was better than him. You know what I said to that, Alma?"

I smiled at her and waited for her answer.

"I told him 'No, I don't think I'm better than anybody. I just know what I'm going to tolerate, and I know especially what I'm not going to tolerate. Alma, he started cussing me out and I very calmly picked up my handbag and I told him that I wish him well and to please not contact me again. I left. Part of me was scared to death because there's that part of me that is afraid of being alone. I questioned myself still, but there's enough of myself that's healed to know that what I did was the right choice. He texted me over and over that night and kept trying to call to apologize. Late that night, he came to my door and was banging. I opened the door and told him to leave and, if he didn't, I would call the police. Alma, I was calm the whole time. I've never been a calm person!"

"What were you feeling when you told him to leave?" I inquired.

"I felt good. It felt right. You know what else I learned? Because, in the past, my behavior was so rotten in relationships, I thought that I deserved that kind of treatment and so, I stayed because I thought I deserved it. I didn't treat this guy badly. I behaved honorably and appropriately at all times. That's what gave me the sense that I was doing the right thing by kicking his ass to the curb!" She reached over and hugged my neck. "Thanks to you!"

The rest of the session was spent discussing how her school was going and how much she really enjoyed her new job. She expressed that she wanted to be able to reach out to me if she needed a pick me up or a "booster shot", as she put it.

"I think I want to stay single for a while. It's not so scary over here. I like me now. Before, I was always trying to get somebody to stay with me and tell me I was a good person and make me feel better about myself. I don't really feel like I need that so much now. I don't mind my own company. I think it would be nice to be in a healthy relationship and I'm OK with waiting for that."

CHAPTER 7

Sexual trauma and promiscuity: Ramon's story

There's a whole host of Generation X divorcees out there in the world, aimlessly and mindlessly navigating the dating scene without a clue. These poor individuals have no idea what they're doing after existing in marriages and relationships, time after time, that have devolved due to lack of loyalty, trust, fidelity, honesty, etc.

Many times, when these clients would present to me, the excuse for their behavior is they aren't "looking for anything serious." Typically, I smile at them and just let them continue to talk. I listen and try not to smile too much. I've heard this story numerous times and I'll hear it again many more times, I'm certain. My job is not to make fun of people, although my clients, for some weird reason, often present with fear that they will be made fun of in therapy. I explain to them that fear is just shame that they've carried for so many years.

Usually, when my clients have exhausted their initial presentation, I will ask them "If you're not looking for anything serious, then why are you dating at all?"

This question results in a variety of responses, from laughter to anger. Many times, clients express discomfort with the question altogether. I try to build rapport by creating a comfort in removing the shame aspect of sex. I'll ask if they're looking for sex only in dating. Men and women equally agree that casual dating for sex provides a sense of comfort and connection without feeling the need to be vulnerable. I like for my clients to have the time and space to express their own interpretation of the point and purpose of dating. The answers range from "I just like to meet new people," to "my ex-husband didn't enjoy sex and now I have an opportunity to figure out what I want and like sexually without the pressures of being in a relationship." These are absolutely valid answers. Generally, I allow clients to utilize the time we share for the purpose of expression of self. Most of the time, when people present initially in therapy, they just simply need someone to actively listen and engage. A huge part of what any therapist does is to be present and involved in a conversation with the client that provides them with the validation of being heard. It never ceases to amaze me how we, as a society, could just help each other so much by simply listening to each other. I encourage my clients in that process to listen to their loved ones as well during their healing journey.

"What do you have in your life that makes you happy?"

This is a question that I often ask clients who come to me for help in their partnerships or dating. Sometimes, it is met with diffusion or a change of subject. Sometimes, clients will answer with a detailed list of everything that they value and appreciate in their lives, to include previous relationships that they learned and grew from. From that perspective, we move into the query of, "Now that you know what you have, what is it that you want?" It is a daunting task to sit down with a therapist and explain what you desire to have in your life. It is a generational aspect of 40-plus year-old individuals, which have been married and divorced, to isolate their own unique desires in life. Many times, this question is met with the answer, "I really don't know. I've never really thought about it honestly."

Midlife dating after divorce can be a total shitshow. I don't think anyone would argue that. It is rife with an endless pool of complicated and damaged participants. So many people in the game out there are trying to date aimlessly, bringing all their old trauma and wounds into new partnerships, expecting a new partner to fix them in some way. What ends up happening is two wounded individuals connect sexually and feel an excitement and attraction and, ultimately, an attachment to each other that feels like intimacy, but is compounded with the expectations of external validation.

Physical intimacy through sex feels great after the dissolution of a disappointing partnership. Unfortunately, without any real connection and communication, the physical intimacy will cease to provide the type of validation that these two damaged individuals seek so desperately. It is the wash-rinse-repeat cycle.

Hundreds of thousands of dollars in attorney's fees later, they will come to me with the expectation of fixing themselves. Fortunately, there is an upside to this. Taking time to get to know yourself, get to know who you are, what you've been doing, why you've been doing it, and what needs to change in order to achieve the desired end result. It's all about you. It has absolutely nothing to do with anyone else. You cannot succeed in finding a healthy and connected partnership if you do not seek to address the wounds you carry.

So, what is it that you have in your life that you want to change? How do you want to improve your life through dating?

What is it about dating and being in a committed relationship that scares you? Do you allow yourself to feel fearful about being in a romantic partnership? Honestly, if you're not fearful about being in a relationship, then that is a huge red flag. We should always have a healthy fear about dating and connection with other people. It doesn't have to be a paralyzing factor but having a general respect in regard for other people and being concerned about how you influence them, as well as how they treat you, is a healthy attitude to maintain in dating. It will continue to provide the levity of how you move through that relationship, by being mindful and aware of the interactions that you keep. If you don't possess a respectful amount of fear in connection with other people then, essentially, that means you're not concerned about how your interactions will affect this potential partner.

It is OK to be afraid. It is important to understand why you are afraid. It is important to understand why you are scared to commit.

It makes sense to casually date as a means of getting familiar with dating again. In fact, if you are recently divorced or out of a long-term relationship, it can be a good idea to date casually. However, dating casually as a means to find sexual partners is problematic over the long term. We all know that sexual promiscuity can result in pregnancy and sexually transmitted infections. However, a lesser-known impact of sexual promiscuity is the emotional and spiritual implications of multiple sexual partners over time. Bear in mind, this is not an attempt to shame anyone for engaging in what feels like a fulfilling sexual experience with many partners. In fact, it is borderline impossible to really understand a person's own intimate sexuality and desire without having several partners over time. However, only you can be the barometer to determine when this behavior becomes emotionally and spiritually problematic.

Are you seeking multiple sexual partners to achieve physical intimacy without the vulnerability of a connected and committed relationship?

Do you feel that your sexual ability is the only thing you have to offer?

Do you enjoy pleasuring your sexual partners as a means of gratifying your own ego?

Are you someone who feels that your sexual prowess is something that should be shared with numerous partners, as opposed to being "wasted" on one long-term partner?

Do you receive your own validation as a worthy human being when other people express a desire to have sex with you?

Have you thought about how long you are going to engage in these behaviors?

Do you logically believe that you will be able to secure sexual partners throughout your entire life, until old age?

Are you fearful of getting into a committed relationship with someone and making another mistake?

Are you traumatized by your past relationships, to the point that you don't want to ever be in a partnership again?

Does this behavior fulfill you?

Perhaps you're not able to find sexual partners, but instead are willing to take whatever is available when it comes to dating.

Are you lonely? Better yet, are you ashamed to admit that you're lonely?

If these questions make you uncomfortable, it is important to understand that you are no different than everyone else. Feeling lonely is a fundamental experience for all humans. Do not believe the hype when you hear people say that they don't need anyone. We all need each other. We all need connection. You are no different. What matters is how you are going about achieving that connection with other people. Do you afford yourself the opportunity to genuinely articulate and value what it is you seek and desire to achieve long term in your dating life?

Are you dating to actually find a long-term partner to care about and for you?

Do you feel that is the purpose of a long-term relationship, is to have someone wait on you hand and foot?

Are you looking for someone to (theoretically) wipe your ass?

Have you considered whether or not you are willing to wipe someone else's ass?

Let's be real. None of us are getting out of here alive. If you are a workaholic who avoids thinking and feeling for the point and sole purpose to avoid the unavoidable termination of this existence then my friend, you will inevitably experience a terrible result.

My goal in writing this book is not only to shed light on problematic personal habits and tolerances in midlife dating, but to provide the reader with permission to step outside of current engagements and to take time for yourself. You need to take time to get to know yourself. Many people of our generation feel that it is a selfish act to do things for ourselves to include taking time to heal from emotional upheaval, such as divorce or the breakup of a relationship. Think of this book as a permission slip to step outside of that mindset and to take time for yourself without the inferred shame or feeling of selfishness that is normally associated with such an act.

Not only are you allowed to take time for yourself to heal and to learn and to grow, but it is critical that you do so at this point. Do you really want to enter into your older, later years as a full-grown juvenile adult who has never taken the time to embark upon a self-journey of love and healing? Perhaps you've never been given the opportunity to learn about who you are and why you act the way you do. Think of this book as a license to grant you this opportunity. I have never in my life, both in my professional as well as my personal experience, ever met a single solitary human being who did not have some type of adverse or traumatic life experience. If you feel that whatever trauma you experienced as a child is so profound and so unbelievably terrible that you have not shared it with a therapist or a counselor or a trusted confidant, then I can absolutely guarantee you that you are not alone. I firmly believe that there is never a story that someone could tell me that would shock me into believing that something that happened to them invalidated who they were as a human being. Absolutely no level of trauma, whether it is physical, emotional, or sexual, could ever cause me to believe that the person that I am working with is worth less as the result of that traumatic experience.

While it is not always the case, infidelity and promiscuity are sometimes the result of unresolved childhood sexual trauma.

Trigger warning Childhood sexual trauma will be described in the following paragraphs in graphic detail. Please skip the following excerpt and move on to the next chapter if you have not yet worked with a therapist regarding your own experiences with childhood sexual trauma and rape.

Ramon was a 54-year-old Hispanic male, twice divorced, with four children. Ramon's divorce from his last wife was still ongoing when we met for our initial visit. He arrived early for his appointment and was extremely professional in his appearance. Ramon was tall and fit. He could easily grace the cover of a magazine. He had a beaming white smile and shook my hand firmly. His appearance and height could be seen as intimidating to some. He was wearing a tailored suit and expensive Italian leather shoes.

"I'm taking a long lunch break to have this visit with you, Alma. It's really nice to meet you finally!" He beamed while taking a seat on the sofa in my office.

"I know we were having a back and forth with the phone calls, trying to get an appointment that worked for both of us. I'm glad to finally meet you as well, Ramon."

"So, I've been talking to my priest and honestly I just don't feel like I'm really into the whole religion thing at all. My mother made me go to mass my whole life. She would get mad at me if I didn't go when I was in college. I used to go just to shut her up. Now, I only go on holidays. I tried to talk to my priest about what was bothering me, but it really just made me more uncomfortable. My colleague, Sarah, said she had spoken with you and recommended you highly. I've never been in therapy before, and I really don't know what to expect."

I responded with, "Totally normal. Many people have never been in therapy and have no idea of what to expect, which is a big reason why they never start to begin with."

We both laughed in agreement. "Why don't you start by telling me what is going on in your life that caused you to reach out for help to begin with. I think that's a good place to start."

Ramon interlaced his fingers, surveyed my office and looked back to me while leaning forward and in a hushed tone stated,

"I didn't tell Sarah why I wanted to see you. She thinks I want to talk to you about anxiety. I guess, in a way, that is true, but I didn't give her all the details."

He paused and coughed into his cupped hand as if to inter-ject an abbreviated pause "Uhm, what do you know about sex stuff?" He inquired in a hushed tone.

"Well Ramon, I know a lot about sex. It all depends on what the context is of your question. Are you having difficulties having sex? Are you having erectile dysfunction issues?"

Ramon busted out laughing "Ha! That's a funny one, Alma! No ma'am. Not here. No problems with my joint!"

I smiled at him and responded with an understanding not of my head.

"What kind of sex stuff are you talking about? Take your time answering. There's no pressure."

I scooted my chair away from him to reach for a bottle of lotion out of my desk. Often, when I can tell that my client is feeling discomfort in disclosing an issue, I will busy myself with a mundane task, such as getting lotion and putting it on my hands. When I do that, it has a tendency to alleviate some of the tension the client may be feeling in expressing a narrative they may not necessarily feel comfortable with just yet. By putting lotion on my hands, I have expressed to them that I am comfortable in the conversation and that I am not feeling any kind of discomfort on their part. I am merely here to do a job and my hands are dry.

Ramon coughed again. "What I mean by sex stuff is stuff that happens to little kids."

"Yes, I am very familiar with childhood sexual abuse. Did something happen to you when you were a child?"

He steadied himself. "Yes and no."

"Is that the reason that you wanted to come and talk to me?" I continued to rub the lotion on my hands while patiently waiting for his answer.

"I've never talked about it. Part of me wants to run out of your office right now. The other part of me wants to sit here and cry. I don't even know if telling you is going to help at this point. I should be over this shit by now. It was 40 years ago. Why can't I forget it ,Alma?"

I placed my lotion back into the drawer and slowly closed it so that it didn't slam shut, as I didn't want to add any additional jarring effects into our dialogue.

"Trauma has no timeline, Ramon. It doesn't dissolve away over time. It stays in our brain as an evolutionary product to protect ourselves. I know you probably don't feel like you're protected, but when we experience any kind of trauma, the effects of that causes us to become hyper aware of any conditions that we can potentially come across at a later point in life to prevent that same kind of trauma from happening again. That's why it never goes anywhere. It's stuck in that reptilian part of our brain, the amygdala."

"I don't know where to start." His jaw clenched.

"Listen, Ramon, I get it. You just met me. You've never been in therapy before. You don't have to tell me anything. This isn't a test. We can spend our time together now and just get to know each other so that you feel safe. We can take time to just build trust. I don't know what happened to you, but I do know that it affected you negatively and deeply. I want you to know that I respect you as a fellow human being and I respect your time and I respect what has happened to you. You don't have to tell me anything. But you are also welcomed to tell me everything. I can assure you that it stays here with me and that I will not judge you. You might be surprised at how positive the experience of sharing your traumatic narrative can be. It's completely up to you."

"Uhm, so you know I told you that I am the creative director of the company I work for, right? So, the truth is that I hate my job. I took this job because my business was failing, and I have bills to pay. Everyone thinks I am some shit hot corporate brainiac who develops all these systems and ideas and I fix all these problems. The truth is, I do, but I cannot seem to fix myself. That has been my lifelong struggle. I am so done with moving through my life feeling like every decision I make is a Band-Aid over the past decision. I want to move forward in my life purposefully and with intention, but I can't seem to get a grip on anything. I'm ready to start living my life the way I want to live it and not the way I feel like other people want me to live it. I don't know how all of that ties into all this shit that happened to me when I was a kid, but I've been reading a lot of books and I think the reason that I cheated on both of my wives and all of the girlfriends in between and that I couldn't seem to keep my dick in my pants, is somehow related to the garbage that I experienced.

I don't know if you can help me with that, but I want to try, and I feel like I'll throw up if I leave your office today without telling you. I don't think I've ever felt this ready and scared at the same time. I just know that it needs to be said out loud and someone else needs to hear it and I need to know what someone else thinks about what happened. No one else knows about it. The only people that know about it are the people who did it to me."

His face was flushed, and he was breathless, as though he had just finished a quick jog.

"Do you mind if we do a couple of simple breathing exercises? I think it would be very helpful, as you appear to be a little bit out of breath, and I want you to feel a sense of calm before you share your story."

Ramon agreed. We sat across from each other, and I demonstrated the deep, diaphragmatic breathing exercises. He appeared to relax.

"Are you ready?" I asked him.

"Yeah. Yeah let's do this." He nodded his head at me.

"Take your time. Whenever you're ready. I'm here." I leaned back in my chair to reflect a relaxed posture.

"Ah. Fuck this is hard." He sighed breathlessly.

"Those mother fuckers. I thought they were my friends. We would go to the basketball court after school. I knew Jimmy since 2nd grade. We were in 9th grade and none of us had to be home until dark. All of our parents worked. We had the full run of the neighborhood. We would play basketball and roughhouse. Sometimes, to avoid having to go home, we would cover for each other while we would go behind the vacant buildings to take a piss or a shit. They were my gang. I was the smallest one of all of them and so I felt protected. Especially Jimmy. Jimmy was weird but he was sort of the leader of our crew. He talked about crazy shit. Sometimes, he would tell us stuff that his dad tried on him. It all makes sense to me now. His dad was messing with him. Of course, you know, we were just dumb ass little kids. We didn't know anything about sexual abuse back in those days. We certainly didn't know how to help him ask for help. Jimmy is in prison now. He'd gone to jail a couple of times before for drugs, but this time he's in prison for rape. You know, Alma, that's when this came back to me, now that I think about it. I saw him on the news. I followed his trial. I hoped that he got the maximum sentence, which he did. 20 years. That little boy was only nine years old." Ramon looked at his shoes as if he was surprised they were on his feet.

"You know what I'm getting ready to tell you, don't you?" Ramon stared at me blankly.

"Go ahead. Whenever you're ready," I expressed to him in a nonjudgmental way.

"So, Jimmy was a big kid. He was tall and he was fat, too. The rest of the kids were kind of average in size for most 9th graders. I guess you could say I was the runt of the group. Figures why Jimmy picked me. So, for some reason we got dismissed from school early that day and I don't know if it was a teacher workday or what, but we were sent home after lunch period. of course, none of us went home. Why go home when our parents wouldn't be home until later anyway? So, we all collected outside near the buses and Jimmy says that we need to go to an abandoned building and hang out. We grabbed our book bags, hopped on our bikes and followed Jimmy. We had ridden our bikes past this abandoned building numerous times, but had never explored inside, even though we had discussed wanting to. I think most of us were afraid to, honestly. Jimmy didn't seem to be scared of anything. So, we followed him into the building after we tossed our bikes near the overgrown bushes at the backside of the building." Ramon stopped suddenly and took a deep breath.

"You're doing a great job!" I reassured him. He nodded at me in agreement.

"Thanks, Alma. I'm OK. I'm going to do this."

He continued. "So, the back of the building had this door that had a shitty rusty padlock on it, but the nails in the door were rusted out, so the door opened pretty easy with one push. We walked inside and there were some old rusty tables and chairs kind of scattered about. There were holes on the wall and graffiti. It smelled like piss. I knew we weren't the first people to come in there. Jimmy directed us into a room next to the larger room where there was a small folding table near the window.

Jimmy started laughing and said, "Hey guys, I got a trick. He preceded to pull his penis out and start to massage it in front of us. I remember feeling uncomfortable and scared, but I couldn't move. I swear to God, Alma, I wanted to run out of there, but I could not fucking move!

Ramon's eyes were wild. "That was when Jimmy came over to me and told me that if I didn't suck his dick he was going to tell everybody that I did. I looked around at everybody else for some kind of a reaction. Brian and Johnny just looked out the window. Jimmy grabbed me and forced me down on to him. I remember thinking that I couldn't breathe. I couldn't believe it was happening. He finished inside my mouth and I immediately threw up. Jimmy started laughing again and said, "Come on guys, let's go play basketball.", I tried to walk, but I was so dizzy and nauseated. Jimmy threw his arm over my shoulder said, "It was your turn anyway. I don't know why you're so upset." Brian and Johnny hopped on their bikes and left me alone there with Jimmy. Jimmy told me that he was my friend, but that something bad might happen to me if I talk about what happened that day. I had never been so scared in my life." Ramon leaned back in the sofa, crossed his arms and preceded to survey my office again. He bit his lip and worked his jaw in deep thought.

"The sad part about all of this, Alma, is that I knew that if I told my parents, it would have killed my mother. My father, well, hell, he was such a prideful man, I really don't know what he would have done. He might have beat the shit out of me for putting myself into that situation to begin with. He might have killed Jimmy and gone to prison. He might have killed Jimmy's dad, to come to think of it. That night after everything happened, I swore I'd never say anything. I thought about killing myself. Matter of fact, when I was in college, I actually tried to kill myself once. Took a whole bottle of benzos and woke up the next day. I was so pissed."

Ramon continued, "I felt so emasculated. I mean, I was 14 years old, and this man forced himself into my mouth. I'm not gay. I didn't like that. It just made me angry. When it came to sex, I became extremely disconnected with people. Sometimes when a woman would give me a blowjob, I would imagine that she was Jimmy. I mean how fucked up is that, Alma?!" Ramon looked at his watch. "Fuck, that hour went by fast!"

"What are you feeling in your body right now, Ramon?"

He took a moment and looked at his watch again, looked out the window and back at me and said, "I feel good. A little numb, if I'm honest. But, I don't feel anywhere near as badly as I thought I was going to."

"Do you ever journal?" I asked.

"Sometimes. I'm a creative director, after all!" he laughed

"Do you think maybe you could take some time each evening and write down your thoughts and feelings? It doesn't have to be a direct relationship to the sexual trauma that you just shared. It can be just about your day and what you're feeling emotionally. The point of journaling is to get to know yourself and to understand the effects of how your trauma have impacted your life. It's completely up to you. I never want my clients to leave here feeling like it is an obligatory homework assignment. But, I will say, that the more you invest in your therapy, the better the outcome will be."

"I can do that." he responded.

"Well let's get you scheduled for next week."

"Deal," he agreed.

Ramon returned next week with a notebook full of notes. Some of them were graphic in detailing the trauma that he experienced. Other points of his journaling revolved around the innumerable sexual conquests he'd experienced over the years. Ramon and I discussed his two ex-wives and his relationship with both of these women. He cried and expressed shame and regret about how he had treated them. He detailed the infidelity as well as his refusal to acknowledge accountability and how he hurt the women he professed to love. We worked together for about 9 months and over this time, Ramon did an enormous amount of heavy lifting, with regards to his sexual trauma, which culminated in his uninhibited promiscuity. We talked about what he desired personally, as well as what he wanted in his future. We talked about his children and new grandbaby. He talked about Jimmy and even expressed compassion for the man who abused him.

"I never expected to actually feel anything but hatred towards him. Jimmy's father had been raping him his whole life. How could Jimmy turn out anything other than what he turned out to be, after having experienced that level of abuse. When I separate myself from the emotional impact of what he did to me and look at everything rationally, it actually kind of makes sense that he did what he did to me. It sucked. It hurt.

It caused me a lot of pain and, as a result, I took that pain out on people around me. I took it out on friends and lovers. I took it out on women who chose to have sex with me casually. But, by and large, I hurt myself the most. I didn't have to turn into a dick and treat people like shit because I was treated poorly. That was my choice."

"Are you still a dick, Ramon? Are you still treating women like shit and using them for sex? Are you still engaging in casual sexual encounters with women outside of your committed relationship?"

"Hell no! Have you seen my girlfriend? She would kick my ass!" He laughed." But seriously. I love this woman. She gets me. She sees me and knows who I really am underneath all the bullshit.

Hell, she was the one, after I started therapy with you, that encouraged me to call up my ex-wives and talk to them and apologize. What kind of girlfriend tells her boyfriend to call his ex-wives and tell them that he's sorry?"

"A good one." I responded.

"I want to marry her but I'm scared".

"What are you scared of Ramon?"

"She's amazing. She's too good for me. I don't deserve her. Yet, she's with me. I am scared that I try it again and I fuck it up again. I am scared that I'll hurt her and then I'll end up alone. Because honestly, she is it for me. There will never be another woman out there that I will feel this way about. I know that."

"If that's true, then why are you scared about cheating? See, the point right now is, you need to work on your own trust. You don't trust yourself and that's OK. You just need to keep working."

Ramon continued to see me for a few more months before he decided he was ready to stop therapy. "I feel like I'm strong enough now and I think I'm ready to start doing some things on my own. I want to be able to call you though, if that's OK, and schedule a session if I hit any road bumps."

We agreed this was a great way to terminate our clinical relationship. He married his girlfriend and started a new business. He was awarded a community service award for the implementation and development of after school programs.

Ramon was a great example for me, as a therapist, to learn from. He was so willing, from the start, to share his narrative and his pain. I know he and I both grew from our clinical connection.

Many times, people with unresolved childhood sexual trauma will use sexual experiences as a tool to process sexual trauma. People who have experienced the disempowerment of sexual assault and abuse can often times feel a sense of empowerment in their sexual connection with other people, as a means to regain something that was felt to be lost through their trauma. The result of this can often be promiscuity and almost an addiction to sexual behavior as a means to deal with the lingering effects of trauma. What better way to take your power back than to remind yourself, over and over again, through endless sexual conquests, that you are the one in control?

Many times, adults who have never addressed childhood sexual trauma will engage in problematic behaviors in relationships, ending in divorce and breakups.

You've heard of the old saying "hurt people hurt people?"

While it's not a justification for the violation of other people, perpetrators of sexual abuse and assaults are often victims of the very crimes they perpetuate. Promiscuity, while not necessarily a crime, can also be the result of unresolved sexual trauma.

If you feel you are promiscuous after leaving a long-term relationship or marriage, you have to ask yourself, "What need am I meeting through this behavior?"

"What is my ultimate end goal here, in engaging in this type of behavior?"

"Is my sexual behavior a problem?"

"Will I be able to engage in a healthy partnership through this type of behavior?"

Experiencing childhood sexual trauma should never be something to be ashamed of. Of course, it's easy for me, as a therapist, to express that to you because I know what I'm saying. The shame associated with sexual trauma comes from having conversations with people who don't know how to respond. Often, trying to share a personal narrative with a trusted colleague or friend can feel incredibly invalidating, particularly when they don't know how to respond to you. Perhaps you trigger something in them that they are not ready to share, as well. Lastly, there will be people out there, if you were to share your story with them, they would absolutely judge you and question whether or not you were the cause of such trauma.

Naturally, none of us want to experience those types of feelings so we tend to shut them down and avoid them altogether.

My hope, for you the reader, in reading this book, is that you will feel validated, if this is your experience. Be mindful of who you share your narrative with, particularly when you're sharing it with someone who might care about you but does not actually possess an educated ability to support you in the way you need. In other words, if you share your experiences with a friend, be mindful that they may say something that seems insensitive or invalidating. Reach out to a professional therapist, particularly someone who has experience in addressing childhood sexual abuse and / or sexual assault. It is an unfortunate, but common occurrence that you should never be ashamed of and that you deserve an opportunity to work through and grow from.

You are not dirty.

You are a worthy human being who deserves to be loved and respected.

If you are behaving in a way that is less than savory, by treating people poorly, I highly recommend that you seek the services of a professional therapist so you can move your life in a direction that is healthy and who will hold you in a space of accountability for your own personal, emotional and spiritual growth and healing.

CHAPTER EIGHT:

Self-worth and kindness

One of the hardest acts to engage upon when a person feels slighted, disrespected, disregarded, or discarded, is to express kindness for that person. When we feel mistreated by someone, our normal human response is to retaliate. We want to make the other person to feel as bad as they have made us feel. When we struggle so deeply to find love and connection with someone else and we are met with the opposite, the last thing in the world we want to do is to project the very thing that we are searching for. It can feel incredibly shameful to be vulnerable to someone that we perceive as attacking us. However, I encourage you to read this chapter from a perspective of growth and understanding.

You've lived enough years on this earth to have the wisdom to know that, what you've been doing in the past, is not working for you. Would you agree with that statement?

Would you agree that the reason for reading this book to begin with, is because you are seeking a new perspective on life and dating? Maybe you picked it up because you had some time to read a book and the cover art grabbed your attention and you thought you might learn something new.

Perhaps a friend recommended this book to you because you have been in numerous relationships that have faltered overtime. Maybe you just don't know what to do next and you're looking for a spark of hope anywhere you can find it.

I would like to remind you, the reader, that, not only am I a therapist, but I am also divorced. I have also run the gamut in the dating game, which was the primary motivator in writing this book to begin with. I believe my purpose here on this earth is to learn and grow and achieve the highest version of my potential. In that process, I feel very strongly that my role is to inspire and motivate those around me that seek the same in their lives. I have gone many years ignoring the fact that I've had a gift to offer others.

This book is my gift to you.

While I may share my clinical wisdom, I am also sharing my personal experiences and my own personal narrative and what it means to learn, grow, and heal from my perspective.

Relationships, by and large, are the outcome of communication.

Nothing more.

Nothing less.

If you struggle to communicate clearly with others, then you cannot rationally expect to have a successful connection. The only person you need to focus your energy on, with regard to dating, is yourself. While that may sound very daunting and intimidating, let's take some baby steps to isolate where your difficulty resides.

First, you must have at least a small amount of willfulness to explore what your habits are and how your habits adversely affect your ability to connect with other people. Making excuses or adopting a mindset of "that's just how I am" can be significant roadblocks in achieving successful connections.

This pertains to friendships as well. To feel the fulfillment of any relationship, romantic or otherwise, there must be an exchange of information in an open and connected fashion.

Recognizing the areas in your life which you can improve upon is critical. I am here to tell you that, the time you take to understand your habits a little bit better (without beating yourself up in judgmental fashion) is a fundamental key toward that goal.

What can you do better?

Do you delude yourself into believing you are not at fault and that everyone you've ever dated has been the problem?

Is it difficult for you to sit with yourself and consider areas of improvement?

I would encourage you to entertain a different way of thinking when it comes to figuring out what you need to fix. So many people get so consumed with the shame they feel when trying to figure out what to do and change. First, when you understand that all human beings are fallible, you can relinquish the shame, you may have associated with any shortcomings you have, perceived or real. When you find an area of your life that needs to be changed or improved upon, knowing that everyone can improve is a mindset that can change your life. This understanding will give you the freedom to make changes without the residual shame that's associated with feeling faulty or broken.

You are just as screwed up as everyone else on the planet.

The people that you perceive to be perfect, aren't.

Everyone has problems.

Everyone makes mistakes.

There is no one on the face of the earth who has all their shit together all the time.

When we adopt a mindset of humility and allow ourselves to feel what hurts, then we can identify what needs to change in ourselves. You may be thinking to yourself "What does all of this self-improvement mumbo jumbo have to do with dating?" The answer is ,"Everything."

Everything you do in life is a direct result of your own cognitions or your beliefs about who you are in this world.

Dating is no different. However, if you have been struggling with connections with other people, then perhaps you are connecting with the wrong people, based upon how you see yourself. We resonate with those who mirror what we feel and think about ourselves whether we do so consciously or subconsciously.

We attract who we believe we are.

We are interested in connections with people that we see similarly as we see ourselves. So, if you believe you are broken and shameful (consciously or subconsciously), then you will attract partners who feel the same way about themselves. You will desire connections with people who treat you the way you believe you deserve to be treated. So, if you have consistently gotten into relationships with people who treated you poorly, chances are, you ignored those red flags in the beginning of your interaction and instead, chose to move forward because you felt like you, on some level, deserved the type of energy you are receiving from this person. If you want to improve your chances to find success in dating, you must first isolate what it is about your own psychological make up that causes you to behave and act in certain ways.

How willing are you to really get to know yourself on the deepest level possible?

Are you ready to face the reality of who you are?

The hardest part is figuring out what you are doing and why.

If you can work past the shame you feel when authentically identifying your own shortcomings, then you will have more power to grow and heal than you have ever imagined!

The possibilities are endless, once you identify and work through all of your own bullshit.

Being single or being in a relationship is irrelevant to your worth. The question is, do you agree with that statement? Often, broken people believe, that in order to feel a sense of worthiness, they must be in a connected partnership with someone else to provide them with the external validation that they so desperately seek. The problem with this mentality is that these relationships very rarely last long term.

When you are constantly working to gain validation from a partner and yet, you do not focus on what you are putting into the relationship, your partner will inevitably become very tired of not having their own needs met. This is not unique to a particular gender, either. Men and women both are equally culpable to these types of behaviors in relationships. It is not just the man's responsibility, nor it is the woman's responsibility, to cater to the needs of their partner relentlessly without any expectation of reciprocity. The concept of self-validation is often an idea that is virtually impossible for many people to grasp. However, it's a beautiful thing to witness in a client, the epiphany when they do realize they have the ability to provide themselves with the validation they so desperately seek to gain from others. This realization is not to invalidate dating altogether but instead to create a sense of worthiness so that you seek the same worthiness in healthy partners in the future. The long and short of all of this is, you really should just get to know yourself before you try to get close to someone else.

Think about it this way. How can you expect your partner to provide you with validation that you do not seek to find within yourself? Additionally, if you do not heal from your own past transgressions and traumas, then you will bring those problems into a future partnership. Would you want to move into an apartment was full of trash from the previous tenant? Would you feel like it is your responsibility to clean out the apartment that you're moving into? Entering into a relationship with someone is no different. Your future partner should not be expected to clean up the messes that you need to clean up yourself. We all have messes too! Let's dig into that metaphor a little bit further. Imagine cleaning up that messy apartment and, as you go through all of the trash, you may occasionally find something of value. A small lamp that still works or a piece of artwork that holds sentimental value, etc. You can value certain aspects of your past without holding on to the residual trauma attached to it. So, when you are doing your own healing, it is critical to pay attention to what you're holding on to and how much value it holds. If that lamp still works and it looks nice, then that's fine. Keep it. But if the lamp is broken and dirty and it doesn't work, but you're still holding on to it, what purpose does that have? Your memories from the past can clutter the future. It's important to identify what's worth keeping and what's worth letting go of.

Who are you?

Many people find this question impossible to answer. Sometimes, people have an answer at the ready, but it's not a well thought out answer. It's an alphabet soup that has been cultivated at the ready, particularly in dating scenarios. The truth is, if we are authentic in answering the question, "Who are you?," we may not be proud of the answer we find. Needy, insecure, overbearing, delusional, angry, hostile, abusive, narcissistic, etc. are not often adjectives that are seen on dating websites. However, many middle aged, divorced people can qualify under a couple of those terms, if not all.

When you stand in the mirror, are you happy with what you see? This query is not just about your physicality, but in relationship to everything that encompasses who you are. What do you have to offer someone in a relationship? If you don't like who you are, are you willing to do the work to improve yourself? Are you willing to become the kind of person that you are seeking to partner with?

All too often, people focus on trying to find an ideal partner without focusing that same energy on an introspective look at self-improvement. Don't you think the person who is deserving of your time, deserves you to take the initiative now to seek out how to achieve your highest potential? Are you engaging in behaviors that will benefit a future partner? Are you taking time to consider the feelings of the person you may spend the rest of your life with by engaging in activities that will improve your cognitions, sense of self, worthiness, and your value? It is much easier to write down the desired traits of a potential partner then it is to identify the things that we need to improve within ourselves.

I would challenge you to write down the desired traits of a potential partner and then use that same list to critique yourself on whether or not you offer those same features.

It is rare that I interact with a client who does not express some form of self-loathing, self-deprecation or self-blame. Sometimes, my clients will openly admit that they hate themselves. I have had clients willingly admit that they do not believe they deserve to find love. Interestingly, I have worked with clients who have engaged in emotional abuse against previous partners, only to realize through their own healing journey, that the reason they treated their partners so poorly was because of their own deeply rooted sense of self-loathing. Because they saw themselves as worthless, they believed the partners in their lives at the time we're equally worthless. If they were not worthless, they would not be in relationships with them. Their subconscious mentality culminated in the projection of that same loathsome mentality towards their partner. If I am worthless, then you must be worthless, too, if you want to be with me. If you are worthless, then you deserve this substandard kind of treatment. Doesn't that make you sad when you think about it that way? It is even more sad when you realize that people don't have to live this way, but they do because they simply do not know better.

All human beings are equally worthy.

No one is better than anyone else.

No one can erode your value or worth.

There is no trauma, assault, abuse, neglect, abandonment, or any other adverse treatment that any one person can perpetuate upon you that can cause you to lose value or worthiness as a human being.

The only person who can erode your worthiness is you.

If you engage in shitty treatment of other people and / or shitty treatment of yourself, then you are eroding your self-worth.

Embarking on an evolution of self-improvement is a challenging task to undertake. It is critical to find clarity in yourself if you expect to achieve the best results in a romantic partnership. Not only should you focus on yourself before dating and figure out what parts of you need to heal, but you must also understand that, just because you are achieving your goals, does not mean your potential partners are doing the same challenging work as well. This is where kindness plays a huge role.

We can do all kinds of self-improvement work to achieve success and fulfillment in dating. We can reach our highest potential and feel the best we've ever felt in our life and yet still interact with people with substandard mentalities, attitudes, and behaviors. These interactions are outside of our control. If dating were easy, everyone would be in a perfect relationship. Unfortunately, the old adage 'you have to kiss a few frogs before you find your prince/princess' is sadly accurate. No amount of challenging work and healing that you do will guarantee you an easy experience in dating. The truth is, not everyone deserves your time. However, to maintain your self-respect and worthiness, it's vital you maintain a personal contract of kindness toward others.

Kindness is a utility. Kindness is a tool. You will never regret being kind, however you can regret treating others poorly.

If someone is unkind to you and you have done a ton of personal growth and healing, it can all come crashing down around your feet if you drop your guard and meet an unkind person with equally unkind behavior. It is difficult to be kind when you have been treated unkindly.

Be kind anyway.

Being kind to other people, particularly when they're treating you in unkind ways, is a demonstration of how far you have come in your journey. It can feel wrong and feel as though you are tolerating other people's unkindness. You should never tolerate unkindness. You can enforce boundaries with people without being unkind. You can refuse to tolerate shitty behavior from others without being equally shitty toward them. It is difficult in midlife to change our mentality on how we handle unkind behavior in others. However, I've seen it done numerous times and I have faith you can do it too. When we understand that other people and their treatment toward us has nothing to do with us, then we can respond to them in kindness, as well as enforce a boundary so that they do not have access to treat us poorly again. It can be as simple as saying, "No, thank you," when someone infringes upon our space or wants our time after mistreating us.

"I understand that's how you feel, but I'm not interested," is a perfectly acceptable response if you're feeling as though you are being manipulated. When we understand how to respond to others in favorable ways after being treated unfavorably, we retain our autonomy and our personal power. We are not allowing other people to manipulate us.

When we can step aside from the unfair infringement, disrespect, name calling, etc., manipulative people have no power with us. This alone will save you an enormous amount of time, when you are able to identify poor treatment with others and respond to it with kindness and boundary enforcement.

Ultimately, you must recognize what you need to change, how to change it, and how to prevent yourself from regressing back into poor behaviors. This life we are living should be purposeful. Not only do you have the right to achieve your highest potential, but you have an obligation to do so, as part of this collective human experience. You are part of something greater than yourself. That is the very fundamental core of why you date to begin with. You are seeking connection.

When you pay attention to yourself and your own areas of improvement, you are increasing your chances of happiness and fulfillment in finding someone equally healed.

Charlie is a 62-year-old retired military officer. He's been married to his wife, Sheila, for 34 years. Charlie came to me asking for help on how to prevent his wife from leaving him. According to Charlie, there were no problems in their marriage and Sheila just suddenly decided she wanted a divorce. Charlie arrived in my office 5 minutes early and was well dressed. He took a seat in the chair across from me opting to avoid the sofa.

"You're welcome to relax on the sofa if you like?" I invited.

"No, I don't need you digging into my brain just yet," He laughed.

"What would you like to talk about today, Charlie?"

"Well, as you know, my wife and I are having some troubles. I really don't know what her problem is. We haven't had any issues until now. I just retired from the Army six months ago. We recently sold our house and downsized into our condominium, since the kids are all grown and moved out. I asked her to come with me today, you know."

"Why didn't she come with you," I asked him.

"She said I was the one that needed therapy. I told her I would go, but I'm not going to keep going by myself."

"Why are you here then? " I asked him. "Do you think you need therapy?"

He laughed. "Of course, I do! But, no offense Doc, you can't handle the kind of problems I have." (I was mildly offended by his negative insinuation regarding my professional aptitude.)

"Well, Charlie," I replied, "if I can't help you, then why are you here?"

"I didn't come here for me. I came here, since you are a woman, to try and see if you can help me figure out what the hell is going on with my wife. We have been married 34 years. We have been together for 36. We were college sweethearts. I thought I knew her. I don't know jack shit." (Again, I made a mental note of the countertransference I was experiencing. I resented his assumption that, due to my gender, I could magically read his wife's mind.)

"What would you like me to tell your wife, Charlie?" I made no attempts to conceal my sarcasm.

"Look, I don't know if you're trying to play games with me or not, but this is a serious situation." Charlie laughed, but I could tell that he was annoyed. He bristled at my statement.

"I'm not trying to play games with you, Charlie. I'm trying to figure out what exactly it is that you need, as well as to figure out the best way to help you."

"Well, if I knew the answer to that, I wouldn't be here."

I smiled at him in agreement. "Charlie, can I ask you a question?"

"Ha! You just did. Might as well ask another one." I ignored Charlie's attempt at humor.

"What did Sheila tell you when she left?"

"She just said she wasn't happy. She said that I don't listen and she didn't feel like I loved her."

" So, what do you think about what she said then?" At this point, I felt that Charlie was starting to relax.

"What do I think? I guess I can speak honestly. I think it's pretty rotten for her to leave me at this point in my life. After all the sacrifices I've made for this country and for her and for our kids, and now she decides that she's just going to abandon us. She decided to abandon me when I needed her the most. What do I think? I think she's a bitch. If I'm being completely honest, I think she's been a bitch for many years now. Repeatedly. Deployment after deployment, she complains. I know she's lonely. I know it's a hard life for a stay-at-home mom to see her husband leave to go to war. But what about me? What about what I've had to deal with? Isn't that what marriage is about? Shouldn't we be able to be safe in knowing that our spouses are not going to just jump ship at any given time? I mean hell, why would she leave now? Why wouldn't she leave years ago?"

"I can sense you're frustrated, but if I may, let me offer up a little bit of validation for you in helping you move forward in this communication with Sheila."

Charlie nodded his head in agreement.

"I know you say that I can't help you or that I don't have the skill set to fix whatever is broken for you, and that may be true, Charlie. However, I do think I can offer up some helpful input to give you at least something to use and work with to improve your current situation with your wife. I want to preface what I have to say to you, by telling you I am here to help, and I am not here to cause you any additional stress. That said, you might feel a little bit defensive with what I want to tell you, but I want you to understand that it's coming from a place of..."

Charlie interrupted me, "Just spit it out. You don't have to sugarcoat things with me. I'm a big boy. I can take it. Tell me all the wonderful ways I'm fucking up my marriage."

"Well first, Charlie, apparently you have all the answers, so I don't know why we're going to waste anymore of each other's time today."

Charlie appeared surprised.

"Listen, I know you don't want to be here, but I also understand the real reasons why you don't want to be here. I know you're afraid to hear that this situation is your fault or at least, part of your fault, anyway. But if I'm going to help you, then you and I need to come to an agreement that we're going to be respectful and that we're not going to talk over each other and that we're not going to insult each other. I'm not going to intentionally cause you any kind of stress or pain, but you also need to understand that I'm not going to sit here and tolerate being talked over or disregarded or disrespected either. Now, can we agree on that?"

Charlie smirked at me. "It's funny, now that I don't have a uniform on, people just talk to me any way they want to. "Sure. Go ahead."

"I think we're done for the day, Charlie."

"Wait? You're kicking me out?" Charlie's tone, while intentional on his part to come across in a demanding demeanor, squeaked by with a tone of pain.

"I am. I am not here to beat you up or make you feel less than. I think I've said that a few times already in the short amount of time we've been in this office. But, you need to recognize my position in my role. Please, do not get my kindness confused with weakness. I've worked with high-ranking officials for several years. If you want my help, then you will be kind and respectful, regardless of whether or not you agree with me. If you cannot follow those guidelines, there's the door because I have other people I can spend my time with helping. I am not going to sit here and beg you to allow me to help you. That's not how this works, Charlie. Now I will ask you one last time, are you willing to sit and listen to what I have to say, regardless of whether or not you agree with me, but will you do so in a respectful tone and posture? I won't treat you any different. I guarantee it."

"I'm sorry." Charlie choked back his tears. "I'm fucking scared. I don't know how to be scared."

"Well, you came to the right place, Charlie. Because I know scared. And if you'll sit there and if you will listen to me, you might learn something. Like you, I've been doing this for a while and I'm confident in my ability to help you. You just need to listen. I'm not here to disrespect you or your service to our Nation, nor am I here to be disrespected. We just need to come to that agreement."

He reached across the table and grabbed a tissue while shaking his head in agreement.

"The thing is, Charlie, you just retired six months ago. Everything about your world has been completely turned upside down. The reason you didn't think there were any problems before, is because you were working and Sheila was taking care of the home and you guys had this agreement, whether spoken or unspoken, in how you were going to manage your marriage and your home and your finances. I can only assume that, when you stopped working, you stayed home and there was conflict as a result. I can only imagine how lost you must feel without being in such a high-level position of authority and then feeling like your entire world has imploded. The changes you are going through right now must feel insurmountable. Allow the fact that maybe, you just don't have the answers on how to fix it and that's perfectly acceptable. That is where I come in."

By now, Charlie had started to hyperventilate because he was sobbing so heavily.

"Big, hardcore, tough Army Ranger sitting over here like a fucking pussy, bawling his eyes out. That's what I'm reduced to." He fought with the box of tissues, grabbing a fistful out angrily.

"Or", I added "perhaps you are a successful retired Army Colonel, decorated from countless combat tours, deployments, and campaigns, who is now embarking on a new chapter in his life that he is simply uninformed about. Perhaps, this is an opportunity to learn and grow in ways that the military prevented you from being able to do in the years past." We sat in silence across from each other for a moment.

Charlie gritted his teeth and set his jaw as the tears continued to flow down his face.

"You know, I cannot remember the last time I cried." Abruptly he shifted in his seat. "Oh wait, yes I do! It was three weeks after my father died. I had just made my first command. I was a brand-new captain. Jesus, that was 23 years ago! I drank a fifth of Jack Daniels and locked myself in my closet. The thing that confused the hell out of me, Alma, was the fact that I hated that motherfucker. When I was a little kid, he used to beat the shit out of me and tell me that he wished I had never been born. He told me I was a bastard because my mother was a whore. My parents were never married because my father could never figure out which woman he wanted to be with. So, on my weekends with my father, I always felt like I was in the way. Occasionally, when he was sober, he would take me outside and teach me things. He taught me how to sharpen the blades on a lawn mower. He taught me how to change the oil in his Oldsmobile. That was fun, because as he was draining the oil, he got oil all over himself. I remember I was scared thinking that he would find a way to blame me for it, but he laughed about it. It turned out to be a great day. But those memories are few and far between. He was a raging drunk with an awful temper. Blah blah blah. I know you've heard all these bullshit stories before. He smacked my mom around a few times. That's probably why she didn't want anything to do with him. I never hit Sheila. I cheated on her once. I came home and told her about it, and she threatened to leave me then. I never did it again, though. That was really early on, and I was just dumb and horny. Truth be told, she probably should have left me back then. I'm embarrassed to admit it, but I was not a good husband. I'm still not a good husband. I'm a great soldier. I'm a hell of a dad, too, because my kids mean more to me than anything. But for some reason, I just couldn't be the person Sheila needed me to be. Alma, I don't even know why she stayed this long." He stared down at the floor.

I let Charlie sit for a moment before I decided to reply and give him my feedback. Usually, when clients present with such authenticity and accountability, they need some time to process the words that come out of their mouth before they can even remotely comprehend anything someone else has to say about what they have just shared. So, we sat together in silence for about 5 minutes. He let out a deep sigh.

"I'm really sorry for being an asshole to you earlier. You didn't deserve that. I think I came in here knowing you were going to tell me that all of this is my fault, and I already knew it. I was just being defensive. I do that to Sheila, too."

"Charlie, it seems to me that you've got a pretty good grip on what's going on in your marriage. I think you are thoughtful, and I think you're self-aware, more than you give yourself credit for. The question moving forward, I think, is to find out what you want to do about it. Do you want to continue being an asshole, as you put it?"

"No, I don't want to be an asshole. I don't want my wife to leave me. I have put her through hell. All these years in the past, I blamed everything on the Army. While it's true, the Army has made me leave my family for months at a time, hell, even a couple of years at a time, I know I leaned into the Army being the reason why I treated my family the way that I did. The Army didn't cheat on Sheila. I did. The Army didn't make me not take all those phone calls when I was too busy goofing off with my soldiers, when all she wanted was to have a conversation with me because she was lonely back home. The Army didn't make me choose to stay late at work every night. I was the commanding officer the last six years I was on active duty, for crying out loud! If anybody was going to set the tone on family time, it was me. Hell, my behavior probably caused a lot of marriages to have problems, because no one wants to leave before the commander does. I set a horrible tone for my married soldiers and their families. All because I was too chickenshit to do what I needed to do for my wife and kids."

"What do you want to do differently, Charlie?" I reiterated my question.

"It's hard for me to ask for help. I have always felt like I should have all the answers all the time. When I was a little kid, if I asked my dad for help with something he would call me a dumb ass and say that I was stupid. He told me real men figure shit out on their own. He told me all the time how worthless and idiotic I was anytime I asked for help with anything. I still feel like that stupid, worthless, little kid now." He stared out the window for a moment. He regrouped and looked back to me and said "I don't think I deserve anything better then what's happening right now."

"Well, if I may Charlie, I think you do deserve a lot more. You just don't know any better because you've never experienced any type of opportunity to heal. You grew up from all of that trauma your father left you with, into a young man working diligently in college and then officer training school and as a commissioned officer learning how to be a good role model, based solely on doing the things that were polar opposite to what your father did. Sometimes, that may have worked to your advantage but overall, I think that you missed the mark on some things. I think now, in your midlife, you're just realizing you can do things differently. You're just frustrated because you don't know how you can do that. I would even go so far as to volunteer the fact that you probably don't even think you deserve to do things differently. Is anything I'm saying to you right now resonating with you? " I asked him.

"Oh, for sure, Alma. I have to tell you, right now, I feel completely and totally worthless. I think Sheila should leave me. I never deserved that woman to begin with. Who the hell am I to try and get her to stay?"

"You're her husband. That's who you are. It's going to take some time and some effort on your part to listen and to be open and vulnerable in understanding how your childhood trauma deeply affected your behavior. It's going to be difficult. I will not lie to you. A lot of your deeply rooted shame will be triggered by the exercises you and I will engage in. You must understand that it is worthwhile to learn and grow and heal. When you learn to look at yourself differently, from a healthier perspective Charlie, you start to see yourself in a way that's not shameful, but worthy. Understand the way you were treated has absolutely nothing to do with your value. As we move on, you will see the experiences you had with your father, while traumatic and hurtful, were simply occurrences because of what your father was dealing with. None of it had anything to do with your worthiness. The things that your father told you about yourself and how he hurt you we're merely lies and abuse. They were inaccurate. It was wrong for your father to treat you that way. He should have been more present. He should have been more kind to you. If your father had been kinder, then perhaps you would learn how to be kinder to yourself. When you learn how to be kind to yourself, then you learn how to express kindness for other people. You learn how to be kind to your spouse."

I looked at the clock and realized we were running out of time. Charlie and I scheduled a meeting for the following week.

"Alma, Sheila left, but we're actually doing a lot better now. She moved in with her sister and, now that we aren't in the same house, we are able to communicate in more respectful ways. I miss her terribly, but at the same time, I also realize I'm getting what I deserve and she's getting what she deserves, which is my respect."

"What are your thoughts about her staying with her sister?"

"I think it's temporary. Her sister needs her help, anyway. It gets us out of each other's hair because, like you said, I just retired six months ago. Neither one of us was prepared for spending that much time together all the time. I think that's really what caused all of this to breakdown the way it did. I hope we can figure out a way to come back together and figure out how we're going to manage our relationship in kinder and more respectful ways."

"Well, from where I'm sitting, that sounds like good news. Is it?"

"I think so. It sucks. I miss having her at home. But I also realize the reason I miss having her at home is because I'm a fucking child. She's always sort of taken care of me and I've always sort of neglected her needs and expected her to baby me on some level. It's funny, Alma. In a lot of ways, I feel like this is the first time I'm actually acting like an adult. Do you know, I have been washing clothes wrong for the past 30 plus years of my life? I know how to wash my fatigues and that's about it. They don't exactly teach you that in the Army." He laughed out loud.

"Have you two talked about divorce?"

"She still brings it up. Two days after I met with you, we had a huge fight. But I was proud of myself because, while it hurt to hear her scream at me, I also felt like I needed it and I felt like I deserved it. In the past when we would fight, I would just return fire and yell at her the same. She would threaten to leave and I would tell her to go ahead. I'm ashamed to admit that I restricted her access to our finances in the past. When she moved in with her sister, she asked me for money and I set up a bank account and I put in a weekly stipend for her to have spending money because she hasn't worked a job in years. I know that was the right thing to do, plus it makes me feel better. I love her, Alma. The thought of her leaving me forever makes me feel like I can't breathe. The kids are grown, and they don't really share their real feelings about what's going on between me and their mother."

Charlie and I would continue to meet weekly for the following six months.

"Charlie, I think you've come a long way. I think it is important for you to take some time to write down all the things you have learned and healed with over these last few months that we've been working together. The most important feature of your healing is to disengage from the self-deprecation that you've been taught to lean into. Understand that you're not that little boy being abused by your drunken father anymore. You didn't deserve all the name calling. Just because your father said that to you, doesn't mean it's true. It just means your father was unhealed and broken himself and he was projecting his own pain upon a vulnerable victim, which happened to be his small son. Look at the kind of father you became because of that. Your children love you and adore you. You're a successful human being by bringing children into this world and treating them with the kindness you did not receive. Acknowledge that as a success for which you deserve to be appreciated. Continue to do your journaling. Continue to do your breathing exercises. Continue to be open and vulnerable in your communication with Sheila."

While he and Sheila reestablished new rules in their marriage, she continued to live with her sister. However, they both expressed a desire to move back in together once they both feel comfortable and ready. Charlie learned how to pay attention to Sheila, because her absence presented him with the knowledge of just how much of an impact her presence had in the home. Sheila was able to appreciate the fact Charlie was willing to financially support her without any argument or constraint. They both learned new and healthier ways of appreciating what each one of them brought to the table during their marriage by engaging in a physical separation. For the first time in over 20 years, Charlie and Sheila went out on dates. He would drive over to Sheila's sister's home, pick her up and take her out to dinner a minimum of three times a week. For the first time in over 20 years, they were dating each other again. They were happy and were enjoying the newfound connection in this new chapter in their lives. Charlie learned kindness was not a utility reserved for just his wife, but also for himself. He learned his self-worth was something he could cultivate with the newfound knowledge he derived in our therapy sessions.

It is impossible to express kindness toward oneself if there is a fundamental lack in self-worth. Charlie was unaware that he felt worthless. He had been able to successfully mask his feelings of worthlessness in his uniform and his positions within the military. When Charlie retired from the Army, all his external validation disappeared. He lost his titles and in having to present himself as he was to the world, he regressed into the small, traumatized child within himself. Charlie's inability to self-regulate and to self-validate caused him to behave in ways that further eroded his relationship with Sheila. Throughout the duration of our therapy, Charlie was able to identify the areas in which he needed to improve and heal. He was able to regulate his emotions in healthy ways and was able to identify his areas of improvement without resulting in self-deprecation. He realized there are healthier ways of learning and growing through our skill building and cognitive behavioral therapy work.

Sheila eventually returned to the home that she and Charlie shared. They continue to check in with me periodically for housekeeping visits, as well as to provide me with updates on how they're doing. Traveling and maintaining a regular schedule of romantic dates has been key to their continued success. Recently, Charlie called to let me know they had become grandparents. Sheila was over the moon. They continue to communicate and treat each other with kindness and respect.

CHAPTER NINE

The Reckoning

Ignorance is bliss.

Have you ever sat down and thought about what that old cliche means?

Naturally, this is a generalization of scientifically proven data. You can rationalize with ease that the smarter you are means you are more aware. Aware of what? Aware of the simplicity of life? Aware of the complexity of how difficult life really is when the fantasy is removed? Human beings are naturally curious. The higher the intellect, the greater the curiosity.

Curiosity killed the cat.

More cliches.

Wanting answers is a normal part of the human experience. We struggle to define every aspect of our lives so we have the fulfillment of understanding. What happens when you move through life though without this curiosity? What if, as a small child, you follow the rules and do as you are told? What if your personality develops based upon the understanding that, as long as you follow the rules and pay attention, that everything in your life will work out to your benefit? What if, as you move through adolescence and early adulthood, you lean into cultural norms, such as finishing high school, going to college, getting a job, starting a family, etc.? When you follow these norms, there is a subconscious expectation of a perceived sense of fulfillment and happiness. However, that is not always the case. In fact, it is often the opposite. As we grow into our own curiosity in early adulthood, or perhaps earlier in adolescence, we become conflicted with our own need for individualized understanding. Our desire to critically think for ourselves is often at odds with cultural norms. Thoughtful, intelligent, willful personality types tend to lean into a more individualized idea of what life should look like, and as such, which decisions should be made based upon these ideals. Problems arise when intelligent people find themselves immersed in a lifestyle that is ungratifying and unfulfilling, due mostly to decisions made prior to the willful engagement of critical thinking.

We all grow into our own personalities at our own speed. Sometimes, people are born into families and social circles that are so tightly knit and woven, that adaptability is key to survival. Critical thinking and individuality can often times be seen as rebellion. Therefore, personal ideals and desires end up being repressed and ignored. People grow up and go to schools they don't want to go to, compete in sports they don't enjoy and even end up partnering and marrying people they don't love.

Many times, people will find themselves living their lives on their own terms away from those previous familial pressures and societal influences, only to realize that the life they have built for themselves is deeply unsatisfying. Regret, at this point, is a common theme, as well as the unconscious sabotaging of professions and marriages as a means of extricating oneself from these situations. How can anyone, in good faith, explain to a spouse of 20 years that they regret marrying them and they wished they had stayed single? How can anyone sit at a desk of a job they have worked at for several years and maintain good standing all while feeling as though their own personal values have been sacrificed as a means to receive a paycheck?

While all of this can be profoundly upsetting, it simply does not have to be.

I have worked with hundreds of clients who have expressed regret over decisions made at a point in their life when they felt they were simply unprepared. Many times, these clients present with mindsets of self-deprecation and feeling as though they are unintelligent and thoughtless in how they have maneuvered through life. Often, clients have stated that they believe they would be happier if they were not in their current condition, profession, or marriage.

The grass is not always greener on the other side. The grass is greenest where you water it.

Cognitive behavioral therapy, in short, is a therapeutic modality which teaches the client how to shift their own perspective and to have different beliefs about who and what they are in the world. It's therapy for a mindset. It challenges unhealthy and unhelpful beliefs and schemas.

We've all heard about the proverbial midlife crisis. It's that magical place in life, when we reach a certain age, we can no longer ignore the fact that we are simply not spring chickens anymore. We have theoretically lived over half of our life. The idea that the best part of life has already happened can be terrifying. People experiencing this phenomenon can make rash and catastrophic life changes. Sabotaging life savings by purchasing expensive sports cars, engaging in infidelity, divorcing a spouse, quitting a job, selling a house, abusing drugs and alcohol, and other dangerous and unhealthy decisions are but a few of the life altering decisions clients have made.

It's a panic.

It's an answer to a gradual understanding about one's own personal experiences in life.

It's a reckoning.

It's also very common. It also does not have to be catastrophic. It is simply the result of a lack of understanding and a need to figure life out. A common metaphor I use to explain what's happening is this; imagine you're on a ship, in the middle of the ocean, on a cruise with your best friends or maybe your partner / spouse and your children. You are having a lovely time. Everything seems perfect. Suddenly, the ship sinks, leaving you and all of your friends and family floating, in a panic. Perhaps some of your friends can't swim and they go under. You are unable to help them because you are trying to keep your head afloat. Perhaps your spouse needs your help, but you're unable to help your spouse swim because you're struggling to swim on your own. There's debris floating in the water that you can grab on to so you can survive a little bit longer.

Struggles and trials in life are no different than this metaphor, when you think about it. When we are struggling, we are unable to help the ones that are closest to us. It doesn't mean we don't want to help them; it just means that we are struggling to survive on our own. When we understand that we are in crisis, we can then assess our need for assistance and help. Imagine another ship coming by with rescue swimmers that come in and pull all of you out of the water and bring you onto the boat to take you to shore. Therapy is much like a rescue swimmer. It is important to understand that, as human beings, we all, at some point in our life, will need some help. It's interesting to note that in this metaphor, many times my clients would have assumed that they knew how to swim and that they knew how to help their partner in that situation, but until you're in the thick of a crisis, you really don't know how you're going to react. Many times, in crisis, my clients will present with feelings of shame. This shame is deeply rooted in the belief that they are the provider and the protector. When the client realizes they are unable to provide that protection at the level they believe they should and were able to, the shame can become quite profound. However, as illustrated earlier, cognitive behavioral therapy is a great tool to help disentangle those feelings of shame from this simple rationalization of where those belief sets came from and why they are inaccurate and unhealthy.

Have you ever sat down and had a conversation with your 80-year-old self?

When you struggle with life at your current age, you might be surprised to discover how your perspective will shift when you redefine what is important to you when your perspective shifts to perceived end of life. Typically, 80-year-olds do not consider the same type of conditions in life that 52-year old's do. Most 80-year-olds have accepted life as it comes, with a full understanding that the clock is running out. Particularly, when that 80-year-old is healthy and active, the concept of mindfulness is paramount. Most 80-year-olds are not planning for 20 years ahead. Instead, they have developed the ability to be in the present. Naturally, of course, the younger a person is, the more important it is to plan for the future. However, that mentality tends to shift in middle age. It can be a daunting task to redefine a person's purpose after having such deeply held mentalities for so many years with regards to youth and the perspective of future endeavors. It is critical to have understanding and compassion for oneself in this transition.

Expression of self-kindness is critical.

Culturally speaking, we are not encouraged to be kind to ourselves. We are encouraged to be kind to our loved ones, but we are socially groomed to be harsh on ourselves as a means of achieving our goals. This harsh mentality can be pervasive throughout life and, if it is not identified, can result in profound depression and anxiety.

What do you think your 80-year-old self would say to you about the decisions you've made in your life so far?

If you have had the opportunity to redefine your personal mentality about self and your worthiness, and if you have the willfulness to be rational in this exercise, I think you might find some pretty interesting answers.

What do you think your 80-year-old self would want you to do at this point in your life?

What decisions do you think you should make based upon how they would affect this future version of you?

Are you focused on the things that are really important?

Are the current ideas you have impetuous in nature?

Are you being irrational and impulsive in how you are redefining who you are at this juncture?

Do you think the decisions you are embarking on at this point in your life are well thought out and timely?

Do you think you have waited too long to make these decisions?

How are your decisions affecting those around you?

How are your decisions affecting those you have engagements with?

Are you being fair to the people you interact with?

Are you being kind to yourself and others?

Leo is a 51-year-old, twice-divorced, Asian American. He and I have worked in the same building for the past four years. Over that time, I was witness to Leo's divorce from his first wife, his courtship of his second wife, and his second divorce. He routinely came by my office to ask casually for my feedback. He is soft spoken with a witty personality. We developed a friendship and mutual respect over time.

Leo expressed a desire to change many things in his life. He was born into a Japanese American family. The cultural implications of his home life indicated that he would go to college and become a successful professional. Leo loved, and still loves his family deeply. However, his desire to achieve his own individual goals were not considered of any professional value. In fact, Leo felt an extreme amount of pressure to avoid any construct of individualism. Leo loved to paint and create with his hands. Unfortunately, this was not considered a legitimate profession by his family. Leo's father was a successful neurosurgeon outside of Seattle, WA. He was the son of a Japanese American who had been incarcerated during WWII for being of Japanese descent.

The familial ties within Leo's Japanese culture were deeply rooted in a sense of pride that cascaded into Leo's profession as a military officer. Additionally, Leo married a lady that his mother approved of. Leo's mother died of cancer during his third year in college. As a means to honor his mother, Leo married the woman she had selected for him. Leo and his first wife managed to stay married for a period of 22 years before Leo decided to engage in an affair with the woman for whom he would leave his first wife. Leo, in his shame, decided the only honorable thing to do at this point was to marry this woman. They managed to stay married for two years. Leo retired from the military after 23 years of active-duty service. He became a civil servant and worked in the building he and I shared. His office was adorned with several beautiful paintings of places he visited over the duration of his military service. He was a skilled woodworker and designed and built several pieces of furniture in his office, as well as his home.

On the surface, Leo appeared to have a relatively positive life. He received numerous accolades and awards throughout his military career. At a glance, it would appear that Leo's life was completely intact. Nothing could have been further from the truth.

One morning, Leo asked me to meet him for lunch last minute. I didn't have any plans, so I agreed to go. We had had lunch several times in the past, but this time Leo had expressed a need to pick my brain. I agreed, as I had not seen him in several months and was just as equally engaged in catching up.

Leo greeted me with a hug. "It's great to see you, Alma." He smiled. "You look great! Here. Have a seat." he pulled my chair out and I sat down across from him. After about 20 minutes of small talk, Leo interjected, "So I have something I need to tell you. I don't know what you're going to say, but just promise me you won't think I'm a complete asshole."

"Well, I can't promise that, Leo." I replied jokingly.

Leo forced a smile that had a sadness to it. "You always make me laugh."

"But seriously, what's going on with you?" I said after realizing that my friend was quite solemn.

"I wanted to meet you here for lunch on purpose because I knew, if I met you in your office, I would lose my shit. Honestly, we may need to leave because I feel like I'm going to lose my shit anyway." Leo waved at the waitress for the check. "Can we go for a walk?"

"Of course."

Leo and I sat in silence for a few moments while we waited for the check to arrive. I could tell by his demeanor and body language that, whatever was going on with him was pretty serious and he needed my attention and understanding. I sat quietly but impatiently while he signed the check and put his wallet back into his back pocket. I collected my bag, we stood and walked out of the restaurant. There was a park located nearby and we walked briskly toward the duck pond, away from prying eyes and ears. After about a 10-minute walk, we situated ourselves on the park bench.

"What's going on, Leo? " I asked with seriousness.

"I tried to kill myself last week." he said earnestly while running his hands through his hair. "I'm a Christian. If I kill myself I will spend all eternity in damnation. I can't seem to shake it. I still want to die, Alma. I don't know what to do."

"Leo, can I hold your hand?" He smiled and reached over to accept my hand. His face was blank and stern. His gaze seemed to be lost and emotionless.

"Leo, what are you feeling right now?" I inquired to understand his current condition.

"Nothing," He responded blankly. "I haven't felt anything in years. I'm tired of living, Alma."

"Leo, has it always been this bad? Have you felt this bad for years?"

"No, it hasn't always been this bad. In fact, I've had moments where I felt happy and alive, but they were fleeting. Honestly, when I think about it, it feels like those moments were torture because they reminded me I had the ability to actually be happy, but not long enough to actually find purpose in life. Now, I just feel like everything I do is robotic and all an act, just to keep people far away from me so they don't see just how hollow and disconnected I really am. In fact, the only reason I wanted to meet with you today was as a last-ditch effort to try and figure this shit out and see if maybe there's something that can be done."

"Have you told anyone else about this, Leo?" I was curious to see if he had expressed these feelings to his girlfriend, any of his children or his buddies out at the golf course.

"Not directly. Not like this. You're the first person I have told directly what exactly is going on with me. I've had conversations with my friends and told them that I was depressed or having a bad day, but we're playing golf. They don't want to hear that shit. Plus, we're all exchanging our own stories about shitty life conditions, health problems, and bitchy wives. No one's really listening to each other. We're just there to disconnect and get away from all of our bullshit. We're not there to be each other's therapist. I don't want to hear about their shit any more than they want to hear about mine."

"Have you talked to your girlfriend about this?"

Leo laughed out loud. "What girlfriend? She left about three weeks ago. I haven't talked to her since. I'm glad she's gone. Now, she can move on in her life with someone who actually gives a shit. I don't care to talk to her. I have no feelings. I have no feelings about anyone. I don't care about myself and I don't care about anyone else. The only thing left is the fact that I know that not caring is not normal."

"Leo, I suspect you know what I'm going to say. "

"Yeah, I know you're not a doc. I know you can't prescribe medications for me. I know I probably need to be hospital-ized. I know I probably need some type of grand gesture in order to get me the help I need. Honestly, I haven't felt like I've had the ability to even get to that point. I don't hate myself. I don't hate other people. I don't love myself and I don't love other people. The only thing I have left in me is the realization that I should have these emotions. I just don't, Alma. I have no passion. I have no involvement and no concern for anything or anyone. It's just numb. I feel like I'm dead already, honestly."

"Leo, will you go with me to the emergency room?"

"I will, but I want you to be honest with me about what to expect. I trust you."

"Well, I can't tell you what the unique personalities are of the people who would triage you in the emergency room, so I can't tell you whether or not you would be treated with respect or dignity. My hope is, that getting to the ER, you will be triaged and seen by a behavioral health specialist sooner rather than later, but I can't guarantee that. I will promise you that I will stay with you. I will make sure that you are treated with respect. I will do everything I can to ensure your needs are addressed."

"Do you think I can be helped?" Leo looked at me for the first time with what appeared to be some semblance of concern. "I'm so fucking tired of all of this. I'm sick of feeling like this. I'm sick of hiding and I'm sick of knowing what I want to do to myself to get out of this spot I'm in."

"I do." I reassured my friend. "I can't sit here and guarantee you what that would look like though, Leo. I just know you are severely depressed and there are medications and therapies that can help you. I'm proud of you for taking the time to share this with me. It makes me feel like I'm doing something right. But, I do know that psychiatric drugs are extremely beneficial for people who struggle with severe depression. It's outside of my wheelhouse for sure. I'm a talk therapist. But, I've also experienced severe depression and I do know that medications are lifesavers."

"At this point, I'll try anything." Leo resigned. He slapped his legs and stood up. "Let's go."

Leo and I rode in silence to the emergency department. I was happy to see he was triaged rather quickly. I was concerned we would be sitting there in the emergency department for hours on end before he was seen. However, we were taken back and, after about 45 minutes of waiting, the on-call doctor came in to speak with us. Leo signed some documents and gave me some help paperwork to hang on to for him. The doctor asked if I needed to leave the room and Leo said, "No. She's staying with me as long as you guys will let her." After a brief conversation of obligatory questions and a suicidal ideations assessment, the doctor conferred with the on-call behavioral health specialist, who arrived within 20 minutes to speak with Leo. Against Leo's wishes, I was asked to leave the room, which is standard protocol. Upon my return, the behavioral health specialist detailed the recommendation to have Leo hospitalized. All his clothing was removed and he was placed into the standard hospital gown and socks.

Leo smiled at me, "I knew I'd end up in the funny farm eventually."

"We're going to get you back on track. Just remember, there's a reason the funny farm exists to begin with. You're not the first person to go through this and you're certainly not the last. You deserve an opportunity to feel better. You can't do this shit on your own, Leo. They're probably going to give you some drugs so you can sleep and then they will set you up with some therapy and get you started on some medications, but again I don't know, I'm just guessing. Just listen to your providers. They know what they're doing."

Leo was wheeled away and waved to me down the hall. "I'll see you soon."

I blew Leo a kiss as he rounded the corner.

Leo was hospitalized for a week and, upon his discharge, was placed in an intensive psychiatric outpatient program for 30 days.

I called the hospital to check on how he was doing with his intensive outpatient program. He was adhering to all the protocols and accepting of all of the medication that was prescribed. Leo, of course, was one of the star patients and excelled in all his therapies. He called me about a week after leaving the inpatient program.

"It goes without saying, Alma, that you're a lifesaver. You know what's funny?"

"What's that?"

"I had forgotten how to cry. I hadn't cried in years and had completely forgotten it. I actually started feeling my feelings in the impatient psychiatric program. The medication they put me on has been helping tremendously. The therapy feels like college all over again, because I feel like I'm in a psychological program. I should have a degree once I'm done," he laughed.

"This warms my heart, Leo," I was starting to tear up myself.

"But in all seriousness, Alma, that shit was scary. I didn't realize how bad it was. I feel better now because I feel. I get sad now and, in a weird way, that makes me happy. It's nice to have feelings. It's nice to have emotions. I just want to thank you."

"Well, Leo, I'm your friend. You would do it for me."

"I absolutely would. It's nice to be able to enjoy life. I don't exactly know where I'm going at this point, but it's nice to know that I have a desire to go somewhere."

"I'm proud of you. I know it wasn't easy." I paused briefly, then asked, "Are you still thinking about killing yourself? I mean, I know we talked about it and you would never do it, but are you still having those thoughts?" I worriedly inquired.

"It's funny that you should ask that. I do still have the thoughts, if I am being completely honest. But, I talk about it openly in group therapy, as well as in my sessions with my new therapist. It feels like I am having to relearn my coping skills. While I know I would never act out on it, I had considered suicide as an outlet for so long that it had become a sort of knee jerk response to any condition that caused me distress. So yes, the thought itself still pops into my brain, but it feels inauthentic, and I am reminded to reframe what it is and what it means to me. It is almost as though it is an intrusive thought and nothing more. I am not legitimately suicidal, just to reassure you."

"Well, that makes me very happy to hear. You sound great, by the way!" I was relieved.

Over the next year and a half, Leo took a leave of absence from his job in order to recover and rehabilitate. He reaches out to me regularly. During his intensive outpatient therapy,

Leo discovered that he had repressed a significant amount of childhood trauma that he had not thought about in over 40 years. He continues to work on himself and his life daily, not as something to just deal with or suffer through, but now expresses a sense of joy and eagerness. He takes his medication regularly, exercises and ensures he is eating well and hydrating appropriately. Leo stopped smoking cigarettes and joined a hiking club, where he met his new girlfriend, Julia.

"I think my mom would have liked Julia. You know, when my mom told me she really liked Joon, my first wife, I think my mom knew that because she was dying, she felt the need to give me positive encouragement so that I could move forward. I don't think she would have cared if I married her or not, honestly. I think my mom just wanted me to be happy. She knew she wasn't going to make it through this cancer and she just wanted to see her son happy. I married Joon because I wanted my mom to be happy. I joined the military because I wanted my dad to be proud of me. I never wanted to serve. I wanted to be an artist. I would have been happy just living in a shack in the woods with my paint and my canvas and my woodworking tools. I love my family, but damn if they didn't fuck me up." Leo snickered. "You know, when my dad died, we cleaned out his house. Do you know what we found, Alma?"

" Tell me." I said

"When I was in college and I would write home, I would always include a drawing or a sketch of something I was impressed with or just thought was beautiful. Do you know that my dad saved all my sketches? I don't know what he did with the letters I sent, but the sketches he kept. He never once told me that he liked my art or my paintings, Alma. I thought he didn't care. It's interesting, the things you learn about your family after they pass away. When we dig through all their stuff, we find out dirty little secrets, the affections, and all that goes with life that we hide away from those around us. It all bubbles up to the surface. Then, we must deal with what that means. It's a reckoning, I suppose. Recreating those relationships based upon newfound information. Realizing who we are based upon the beliefs we had, that are now dissolved because of those discoveries. Now I wonder if my father even wanted to be a doctor himself. What was it about becoming a doctor that made him feel seen? I wonder if he went to medical school to make his father proud the way that I went into the military to make him proud. These are the questions I have and these are the questions I will never get any answers to. It's OK though. I know who I am and I know what I want and I know that I deserve to live my life on my terms, finally."

Leo's story is not uncommon. Many people struggle with crippling depression and anxiety during midlife. It can feel embarrassing to ask for help, particularly when you feel like you're the only one who feels that way. The experiences we have in our life are abstract and organic. There is no right or wrong answer for how any one person can manifest their own reality. When we achieve half a century of life wisdom, there can be a subconscious expectation that, through that wisdom, we should also have the ability to figure out our problems on our own. The problem with this philosophy is that depression is a liar.

Depression crawls into your soul and makes you believe things that aren't true.

Depression makes you feel like there is no hope.

Depression deceives and manipulates you into believing you do not have the tools to figure out a way out of it.

Depression is confusing.

Depression steals not only your joy, but your energy.

Not only do you lose the ability to fix your problems, but you lose the willingness to even try. This is why it is so critical to reach out and connect with other people. This is why it is critical to find those who are skilled in not only assessing the critical features of depression, but also the ability to intervene.

CHAPTER TEN

The End; Mike and Donna

The end.

Dying.

Death.

Fear of the unknown.

There are a lot of unknowns in life.

We all try to navigate the murky waters of our existence in a variety of ways. Some of these ways can be perceived as being healthy and some, not so much. We can practice healthy habits like eating right, drinking water, and exercising. We can also use drugs and alcohol to mask our pain, trauma, and anxiety about our fears. We all must metabolize how we interpret our environment through the lens that we've grown into. Some of us may have learned how to deal with our fears in angry and aggressive ways. Those ways have, undoubtedly, negatively affected our ability to interact with other people, let alone participate in healthy intimate partnerships. Some people effectively delude themselves into denial of the fear altogether.

However, exposure to other environmental experiences can undo do some of these delusions, albeit temporarily. How do you feel when you're driving to work or to school or running an errand and you encounter a funeral procession? Do you get that lump in your throat and consider consciously, "That will be me one day?"

Do you ever drive by a cemetery and consider the stories of the people who rest there?

Do you ever wonder how they lived their lives?

Do you ever wonder who loved them or whether they lived their lives devoid of companionship and connection?

We can't get away from the inevitable. We can deny it and ignore it and pretend that it's not there. For many of us, particularly in the first and second half of our lives we may have been able to successfully avoid the contemplative nature of our final chapter in this realm. However it seems to me, all that really does is leave the residue of a life not quite fully lived and instead, create unnecessary hardship for those we leave behind.

Some of us may leave this earthly existence suddenly. Accidents happen every day. We are rushing in and out of our responsibilities, back and forth between places, people, and things. We lose people all the time. Some people may get a dire health diagnosis and may languish for years before passing on.

Of course, this is an uncomfortable topic. No one wants to consider their own demise. But if I may interject some considerations, you may find that taking the time to articulate how you want to live this life fully and with direction and purpose, may essentially alleviate any of your potential regrets at the end of your story.

How do you want to live your life?

Are you actualizing your potential?

Are you learning the things you want to learn in the here and now?

Are you living your life based upon the expectations of others without any real consideration for what you want to be and do?

Are you loving people the way you want to love?

Better yet, are you being loved the way you want to be loved?

How deeply are you willing to dive into yourself to investigate who and what you are on your own terms, without the external influence of your culture, family, and friends' circles?

These are the questions that need to be answered for you to move forward in your life mindfully and with the depth of purpose that you value as an individual.

Right here and now, as you're reading this book, you are empowered with the ability to choose. You can identify the direction you're moving in this life is the one that is going to be the most fulfilling.

I don't think anybody goes through life feeling like they have all the answers all the time. It is a facet of the human experience to fail, make mistakes, change direction, and change your mind.

For those of us in what is considered the middle part of our lives, it is probably a more difficult concept due simply to the timeline of how long we have been doing what we've been doing that has not been working in our lives.

Meditation is a key factor in slowing down and taking time to really understand how you're thinking and feeling, and how your thoughts and feelings affect your actions.

Just because you have been conducting your life in a particular fashion for an extended amount of time does not negate the power you have for change. You can start right now by closing this chapter and simply taking one long deep breath. You get to decide how you're going to live your life, starting right now. Change can be terrifying, but when you can articulate what it is that you need to change, the decisions ahead of you will start to make themselves. If your normal process and habit is to wake up in the morning and immediately kick start your day without any consideration or intention, your life will not be guided by you, but instead your obligations of the day.

Here's another metaphor to consider.

Rational people will consider the speed in which they are travelling when on the highway prior to taking an exit. Anyone who operates a vehicle knows that you must slow your speed before you can safely take the off ramp on the highway. Operating your life is no different. If your alarm goes off in a jarring fashion every morning, it will set the tone for your day. If you turn off your alarm and immediately jump out of your bed and initiate your normal morning routine, then you haven't effectively given yourself time to consciously focus on the purpose of your day. This is the first step to change. If you want to take a different direction in your life, you must first slow down as though you're driving a vehicle on the highway and you are anticipating an off ramp ahead.

The hesitation, anxiety, or even fear you may feel when encountering that funeral procession or driving by a cemetery, can easily be minimized through a meditative practice. That anxiety you fear and feel when encountering the unwelcome thoughts of death and dying can possibly be a result of regret. It maybe a result of questioning whether or not you have achieved the goals you desire. It may even be the result of feeling you don't even know what your goals ever were to begin with.

Many people subconsciously satiate this confusion with unfulfilling and superficial relationships with other people to allay their fears through a distraction.

It is scary to be alone.

The thought of death and dying can magnify this fear. So, if you're swept up in fear all the time, you're more likely to reach out and connect with whatever is available in your sphere. It doesn't mean you're a bad person. It just means you're human.

Many of us have witnessed the languishing of a loved one prior to their death which exacerbates our fear of our own demise. Perhaps, in the experience of taking care of a loved one through their own dying experience, has provided you a sense of comfort with the understanding of what it looks like from the outside. Maybe through this experience, we are able make up our mind on how we choose to leave at the end of our final chapter.

With all this discussion of fear and death and dying and all things dark and scary, comes the understanding that life is to be cherished and lived fully without reservation. We all come here into this space to learn and grow in love. Sometimes our fear becomes so overwhelming that our ability to fully love others is muted to the point where we are merely surviving life.

That's the whole point of this book.

Life does not have to be scary!

Life is meant to be shared in connection with those around us. Our relationships with loved ones is the sole purpose of why we're here. We do ourselves a great disservice when we don't acknowledge our own need for connection and love. When we subconsciously mute our ability to be vulnerable to those around us, we inadvertently disconnect from the ability to genuinely partner in a deeply satisfying connection. We must be willful. We must understand our habits and our fears so we can make healthy changes for a more satisfying future.

So, if we go through life using and, in some cases, abusing other people, we simply cannot expect to have a healthy outcome in our connection with others. Life does not work that way. The level of love and vulnerability you are willing to engage in the universe is a direct reflection of what you will receive. If you throw a tennis ball against a wall, you can fully expect a tennis ball to return to you. If you are putting forth manipulative behaviors, toxicity, and using people for your own advantage and benefit, then you will only receive the same level of dysfunction in return.

It isn't a point of self-deprecation, but a point of self-observation to identify whether or not your habits are healthy or unhealthy in the engagement with those around you. Today is quite literally the first day of the rest of your life and is the perfect opportunity for you to address your own behaviors and to incorporate healthier ones in the future.

It's hard to admit fault, particularly when our behaviors and habits have negatively impacted those around us especially if those are the people we profess to love and care about. It is critical you take time to slow down and meditate on what exactly it is that you need to change in yourself. Once you have identified what you need to change, you need to identify how that behavior has affected those around you. If you need to apologize and be accountable to other people, then that is what you should do. You should also provide accountability in those situations without any expectation of forgiveness or any type of reward.

You should always go into an apology without any expectations. Expression of an apology should culminate from a sense of accountability and nothing more. Look at it this way, you are growing. You are healing. This is a journey. To be able to hold space and step outside of your own protective ego and do what you need to do to correct a mistake or misstep, is a deeply honorable action. It can be incredibly intimidating to allow yourself to be vulnerable to your shame trigger. It is embarrassing to say you were wrong. It is an incredible act that demonstrates a depth of character to be able to demonstrate the intestinal fortitude of accountability. Imagine how incredible it feels on the other side of developing the strength of character to be able to identify a misstep and also to be able to be accountable to that? Isn't it awe-inspiring to consider the ability to be able to emotionally regulate yourself to the point where you are no longer triggered by your shame? Isn't it amazing to consider that you have the ability to right a wrong and not feel as though you are that small child yet again being shamed?

You don't have to feel shame.

Shame is never yours to carry, particularly when it was something that was handed to you as a child. In fact, the only time you should ever feel shame is when you aren't accountable for your own missteps, and not for what someone else has done or said to you.

Additionally, if someone does not want anything to do with you after you have harmed them then you can also learn how to accept that at face value.

Accountability is critical to moving forward.

Accountability is critical in assessing your own fear and shame.

It sucks to admit we are wrong, but when we do so we elevate ourselves into a higher version of who we are. Our value of self increases, whether we realize this consciously or not. Changed behavior will increase the quality of your life and will lower the instance of the anxiety you feel when you are confronted with reminders of the terminal aspect of this existence.

Slow down.

Think.

Ask questions of yourself.

What do you want moving forward?

Accountability is the root of all forms of forgiveness, to include forgiving yourself.

After all, there's a whole lot of life left to live. Do you want to continue living your life and making the kinds of decisions you have been making or do you want to do things a little differently?

It's exciting when you think about it, isn't it?

Taking stock of who you are at this point in your life and being grateful for the opportunity to continue living. It is a tremendous gift that, despite any errors you may have made in the past, you have this beautiful opportunity for growth.

When you look at that cemetery you must realize that time is up for what those people wanted.

You're still here.

You get to choose and make healthy decisions about your relationships and the kind of person you want to be moving forward in this life.

Date yourself.

No, really. Take yourself out on dates. Get to know yourself.

Do you like who you are?

What is about you that makes you attractive to other people?

It's OK if you can't find any redeeming qualities that set you apart from others in your peer group. Now is the time to develop into the kind of person that you want to be. After all, we attract who we are into our lives. If you don't want to attract someone who's just like you, then it's time to start doing that work.

There is no better day than today.

There's no better time than right now.

You don't have to live in fear. You don't have to worry about the end of your life all the time. You can be mindful and grateful for having this moment, right here and right now. You can achieve your goals in personal growth and set healthy boundaries about what you will and won't tolerate in your interpersonal connections with others.

You can learn to see yourself as a worthy person who deserves to be respected and appreciated and loved to the degree with which she wished to receive.

My client, Donna, passed away at the age of 56 from breast cancer. I can recall the first time I met her, how much she reminded me of the actress Sissy Spacek. She spoke with a southern twang and had beautiful long, straight, strawberry blonde hair. Her fair complexion was complemented with freckles and a bright white smile. She was my client for about 18 months.

Donna struggled with her grief after losing her husband, Mike, to heart failure six months prior. Her sunny disposition, while comforting to those around her, seemed to be a disadvantage to her being able to properly address the sadness she felt. It took a couple of visits before she was able to connect with her grief and cry openly in front of me during our session. I reassured her that being sad was perfectly acceptable and she was entitled to mourn the loss of her sweetheart. She was married for 25 years to her high school sweetheart. They met in church and he was the only man she had ever had sex with. Her husband, Mike, had developed a heart condition and had to retire early from the railroad. Donna was a hairdresser and supported Mike and their two girls when he came home. Mike's health continued to decline and, six months after leaving his job, passed away in his sleep from heart failure. Donna was a grieving widow when I first met her, but her resolve was absolute. She missed her sweetheart deeply, but I had noticed our conversations we're always centered around their happy times together. Their oldest daughter, Chelsea, had Down syndrome. Mike was always present and encouraging with her, particularly when she first started school. Their younger daughter, Melissa, was a star athlete and participated in drama class. She was always putting on plays or doing acrobatics in the front yard. Donna detailed all the many times that Mike would come home from work and would take time to watch Melissa show him a new flip she had taught herself or a new play that she had written. Chelsea would always want to cook with Mike,

Donna detailed in her normal bubbly fashion. She told me about their early days in dating. Mike would break up with her and they would get back together and then Donna would break up with Mike and then they would get back together, but they would always seem to find their way back in each other's arms.

When I first met Donna, I was sad for her having lost the love of her life. However, Donna never expressed any self-pity. She would cry and grieve in my office, but through her tears, she would always remind me of the stories and the love they shared. Donna was always quick to make sure that her narrative was not upsetting to me. I would routinely reassure her that this was her time and she was not an inconvenience. Donna thoroughly enjoyed talking about Mike. During one of our sessions Donna tearfully professed, "I feel like I can never talk about him! I feel like if I bring him up, that it's upsetting to whoever I'm around so I don't ever talk about him, Alma." Donna reached over and patted me on the knee. "You sure make me feel comfortable. You're good at what you do," she said smiling through her tears.

"I'm your therapist, Donna. I want to know how you're feeling. I want you to have the safety to say whatever you need to say. I also want you to understand, you might want to reconsider how you feel about talking about your husband in front of your friends and family. It might actually make them feel a little bit better. What do you think about that?"

"I don't know. I just feel like if I bring it up, that I am depressing everybody around me. It's weird." She confessed.

"Well, look at it this way. It might be possible your friends and family are simply waiting for you to bring up the topic so they can talk about Mike with you as well? How would it make you feel if your friends and family wanted to speak with you about Mike? Would it upset you?" I inquired casually.

"Oh gosh no! I would love it if they would bring it up. I would love to talk about Mike more! We all just seem to try to kind of avoid it."

I reassured Donna that it was quite alright for her to engage her friends and family. "Everyone is grieving," I told her. "They miss him too. I think they might be waiting for your permission."

Donna agreed.

She and I talked quite often over the next several months. I learned a lot about her and her children. Mike was a quiet man whose love language was acts of service. Donna told me a funny story of how the tiles in their bathroom had started to crack and chip away. One time, she told me how she was standing naked in the shower and flicked one of the tiles with her nail and half of the wall fell at her feet. She was having a terrible morning getting ready for work. She had to finish getting ready in the sink. That evening, returning from her salon, she came home to find that Mike had taken the day off from work and had completely redone the entire shower.

I asked Donna what she planned to do with her future. "Well, I got to get these girls through high school first and after that, college. I got a little bit of money in savings and Mike and I always wanted to go to Iceland. I think that's the first thing I'll do."

"When do you plan to go to Iceland?"

Donna smiled at me "Not sure just yet. I've got my own health issues to think about right now. Once I get the girls settled, I'll make some plans."

Donna and I continued to visit for another six months. During that time frame, she had received her breast cancer diagnosis as well as her terminal condition. While she was unhappy with how her health was progressing, she never faltered in her gratitude. I was deeply impressed with how she was maintaining her mindfulness despite her declining health. Donna planned for her best friend and her husband to become guardians for their daughters after her passing.

I often think about Donna, her demeanor, her attitude and her perspective on life. Many of my clients would find that Mike and Donna's existence somewhat unexciting, perhaps even boring. Being in a committed relationship with one person for your entire life is something that is a daunting construct, particularly now when instant gratification is reinforced through social and mainstream media. Our values are based upon a fear of missing out. We want to have it all with as many people as possible. But our time is limited and that presents an issue when it comes to developing relationships that have depth. Mike and Donna didn't fight a lot. They were very sweet and kind to one another. They never cheated on each other. They were the epitome of a loving, sweet, kind, and caring couple. They moved through life in a way most people don't see much of these days. And despite the challenges they faced as a couple raising two daughters, one of which was born with a significant disability, they still managed to create a deeply satisfying relationship. They set an example, not only for their children, but for all their friends and family.

Do I think everyone has the capacity to develop a relationship like Donna and Mike's? No, but that doesn't mean we cannot have healthy connections with those around us by making good decisions that are mutually beneficial and not from a place of manipulative tactics or toxicity.

Should you date someone just so you can find someone to wipe your a**?

Should you date someone just so you have somebody with you at the end of your life?

Of course not. Our relationships should not be based in an expectation of a particular outcome or behavior, but instead provide the depth of connection where the safety of having that kind of support can be found. No, you shouldn't date to find somebody to wipe your a**, but you should date somebody you can develop a deep connection with, who doesn't mind doing that for you. You should date someone you can see yourself wiping their a**, as well.

No one's getting out of here alive.

You might as well make the best of it now.

Be grateful.

Be kind.

Be mindful.

Learn how to love yourself.

Go love someone without reservation.

Be vulnerable.

Don't be scared.

Listen to your gut.

Your intuition will never lie to you.

CONCLUSION

Time.

That's really all we have.

Time is our most valuable commodity.

Some of us only have a few moments while others are gifted decades of healthy years. The catch is, no one knows what they're given.

We can't read other people's minds. The only thing we have to work with is our own interpretation of the world around us. We can affect the world around us through our own behavior.

I believe we are here to learn a lesson. Regardless of what your spiritual beliefs or path is, I believe you and I were meant to connect through this book. I believe you and I share a journey, even if we never meet face-to-face. I believe the commonalities you and I share as human beings and the experiences we have had, are far more similar than what we will ever comprehend.

The truth in all of this is that none of us know anything. Isn't that the point though? If we were born into this world with all the answers, what's the fun and purpose in that?

Ultimately, if we give ourselves the time to sit and genuinely consider what it is about life that makes us, us, then I think that we will resolve our own curiosities about our purpose.

My philosophy is that the complications and confusion that comes in life is when we hold other people accountable for what we expect life to bring us. There's nothing more frustrating than attempting to cultivate an attachment in another person when that other person does not share a common interest or value. That's what makes human relationships so complex and, at times, hurtful and unfulfilling.

My goal in writing this book was not to convince people they should date for long-term commitment. My motivation in writing this book was to provide some form of external validation in the fact that, not only is it appropriate, but it is your responsibility to characterize your life on your terms by critically thinking about what is important to you as an individual.

So many people get lost and enmeshed in attachment style connections with other human beings with an expectation of safety and security. While that may be true to some degree, it often leaves us wondering about what our worth is in the eyes of this other person. Being a therapist has given me a unique lens into the mindset and insecurities of individuals who are in committed partnerships and / or questionable situationships. There is turmoil, grief, insecurity, pain, regret, betrayal, and a host of other negative toxic traits attributed to the irresponsible willfulness' of people who attach themselves merely for the gratification of simply not being alone. All relationships are messy to some degree. We come into this world dealing with caregivers who are ill-equipped to provide us the type of nurture and safety into which all human beings should be brought. We learn to characterize ourselves through the lens of a broken caregiver. We grow up and adapt to the mentalities of those broken people around us. In reality, what we should be doing is allowing ourselves to grow and adapt in healthy ways in an unhealthy environment.

My hope is that this book will provide you with a sense of direction that works for you as an individual. My hope is that it has provided you with a sense of validation so that you know, moving forward, you can do so with purposeful intent that will hopefully alleviate the majority of the pain associated with unproductive connections with other people.

We all have to heal and grow.

We all have to assess who we are as individuals before we can even begin to enter into a healthy connection with someone else for the long term.

A connection based upon an expectation of a reward is, in and of itself, unfair and unhealthy to both partners.

It's easier to communicate with other people when you know what you're saying to begin with. You will only know what you're going to say when you know what you think and feel. You only know what you think and feel after you've given yourself time to understand yourself.

No one likes to be alone, but like I said at the very beginning of this book, we all come into this world alone and we are all going to leave this world alone.

Genuine, authentic joy comes from the realization of just how fragile life really is. When you develop an appreciation for the fragility of life, then you're well on your way to an authentic connection with someone else.

However, should you reach a point in your life where you can no longer take care of your own personal hygiene, my hope is that you are encircled by those who love you and are committed to ensuring you have what you need at any given time.

Make sure you are acting and engaging those around you in ways that encourage those people to want to be there for you. It's not always easy to be a good person. It's not always easy to do the right things and make good choices. It's a scary proposition to look back on the past and acknowledge our own shortcomings.

Take a moment to sit back and think about that little boy or little girl that lives inside you. What does he or she deserve? It takes a whole different tone when you look at it from a third-party perspective. You still have time to be your own hero. You still have time to do the work.

You still have time.

Inherently, you are a valuable and worthy person deserving of love, empathy and compassion. I encourage you to engage upon that deep-dive personal introspection to figure out what you need to change, fix and do.

On a humorous, yet serious note, I hope that you are always able to wipe your own ass. But if not, I hope that you are always surrounded by those who don't mind wiping it for you.

I wish you love. I wish you peace.

Alma